ST. FRANCIS OF ASSISI PREACHING TO THE BIRDS.
(*Giotto.*) See pages v. and 43.

The Church and the Animals

Catholic Authors Press
Hartford, Connecticut

www.CatholicAuthors.com

Nihil Obstat:
> GULIELMUS H. KENT, O.S.C.,
> > *Censor Deputatus.*

Imprimi Potest:
> GULIELMUS,
> > EPISCOPUS ARINDELENSIS,
> > > *Vicarius Generalis.*

WESTMONASTERII,
> *Die 13th October,* 1906.

Copyright 1906
Catholic Authors Press Edition 2005
ISBN: 0977616843
Previously titled The Church and Kindness to Animals

ST. FRANCIS PREACHING TO THE BIRDS.

Eat not greedily:
Sometimes, for sweet mercy's sake,
Worm or insect spare to take,
    Let it crawl or fly.

Sing ye not near
To our church on Holy Day,
Lest the human folk should stray
    From their prayers to hear.

Now depart in peace;
In God's name I bless each one.
May your days be long i' the sun,
    And your joys increase.

And remember me,
Your poor brother Francis, who
Loveth and thanketh you
    For this courtesy.

Sometimes, when ye sing,
Name my name, that He may take
Pity for the dear song's sake
    On my short-coming.

Contents.

	PAGE
CONDEMNATION OF BULL-FIGHTING	1
ANIMALS IN THE LIVES AND LEGENDS OF SAINTS	19
A CLOUD OF MODERN WITNESSES	137

Illustrations.

St. Francis of Assisi Preaching to the Birds. (*Giotto.*) Page 43. *Frontispiece.*

St. Antony of Padua Preaching to the Fishes. (*Gerard David.*) Page 49.

St. Hubert's Vision of the Crucifix in the Horns of the Hunted Stag. (*Dürer.*) Page 63.

St. Giles Receiving through his Hand the Arrow aimed at the Hind. (*Flemish School.*) Page 97.

St. Giles, an Athenian, came to France, and lived as a holy Hermit in the Forest of Nismes—a name of good repute among friends of animals, since it was a Bishop of Nismes who wrote the protest, printed elsewhere, against the introduction of bull-baiting into France. The Hermit made friends with a hind, who was one day hunted by a Prince; and the Prince's arrow the Hermit intercepted with his hand.

St. Jerome Companioned by Animals. (*Dürer.*) Page 129.

St. Jerome is commonly shown in Art with a lion, about whom there is the legend that it companioned and guarded him in return for his having fearlessly extracted a thorn from its paw. A second beast (sometimes mentioned as a donkey, sometimes as a lamb) is assigned to the Saint's companionship and to the protection of the lion.

St. Anthony the Hermit and his Hog. (*Nicolo Pisano.*) Page 193.

Condemnation of Bull Fights.

One lesson, Shepherd, let us two divide—
Never to blend our pleasure or our pride
  With sorrow to the meanest thing that feels.

WORDSWORTH.

The Church and Kindness to Animals.

POPE SAINT PIUS V.

"*De Salute Gregis.*"

The forbidding of the baiting of bulls and other beasts; and the nullification of promises and bets contracted at such baiting.

Pius, Bishop, Servant of the servants of God, for the continual recollection of the matter. Concerning the safety of the flock of our Lord, entrusted by divine superintendence to our care: According as we are constrained by what is due to our pastoral office, anxiously pondering over the matter, we are desirous of keeping all the faithful of the same flock not only from imminent danger to the body, but also from everlasting destruction of the soul. It is true that the abominable custom of duelling, invented by the Devil, that, by the bloody death of the body, he may bring about ruin of souls, was forbidden by the decree of the Council of Trent, but, nevertheless, even now in many States and in divers places very many men do not cease to assemble with bulls and other wild beasts, both in public and private exhibitions, for the purpose of displaying their own strength and daring; hence men meet with death, broken limbs, and danger to their souls. We, therefore, regarding these exhibitions, where bulls and wild beasts are baited in the circus or Forum, as being contrary to Christian duty and charity, and desiring that these bloody and disreputable exhibitions of devils rather than of men should be abolished, and that we should take measures for the saving of souls, as far as we can, under God's help, to all and individual Christian Princes who are honoured with any rank, whether ecclesiastical, civil, or even Imperial, Royal, or any other, by whatever name they are called, as well as to all people and states (desiring that these injunctions should be established by our decree for ever under the threat of excommunication and anathema, on incurring the penalty), prohibit and forbid to allow in their provinces, states, lands, or towns and other places, exhibitions of this kind where there is baiting of bulls and other wild beasts. We forbid soldiers and all other persons, whether on foot or on horseback, to dare to contend with bulls or other beasts in the aforementioned exhibitions. And if any one of them meets with his death there he shall be deprived of Christian burial. We likewise forbid the Clergy, whether regular or secular, who hold office in the Church, or who are in Holy Orders, to be present at such exhibitions under the penalty of excommunication. And all debts, obligations, and bets by whatever persons contracted, whether from universities or colleges, with reference to bull-baitings of this kind, even supposing they themselves wrongly imagine them to be held in honour of the Saints, or of any ecclesiastical anniversaries or festivals, which ought to be celebrated and honoured with godly praise, spiritual joy, and words of piety, all such, whether contracted in the past, present, or future, we altogether prohibit and annul, and we decree and declare in perpetuity that they are to be held void and of none effect. We issue our command to all Princes, Officers, Barons, and those who hold rank in the Holy Roman Church, under penalty of deprivation of the rank which they hold from the Roman Church itself; but all other Christian princes and lords of land, to whom our commands have been given, we exhort in the Lord, and order, in virtue of our sacred right to obedience, that out of reverence and honour for the Divine Name, they most carefully honour and cause the foregoing to be observed in their dominions and lands, seeing that they will receive the richest reward from God Himself for such good works. And to our Venerable Brethren throughout the world, Patriarchs, Primates, Archbishops, Bishops, and other local officers, in virtue of our sacred right to obedience, under the solemn thought of the judgment of God, and the threat of eternal curse, we command that they cause our present letter to be published, as far as possible, in their own states and dioceses.

(*Given in Rome at St. Peter's in the Year of Our Lord, 1567, the Kalends of November, in the second year of our Pontificate.*)

Bullarium A Greg. VII. usque ad S.D.N. Sixtum V. Pont. Opt. Max. Romæ, 1586.

MONSIGNOR BESSON, BISHOP OF NISMES,

On Bull Fights and Games.

There was a time, dear brethren, when Bishops were listened to with the attention due to their words, and obeyed with the docility and zeal called for by their Divine mission.

This was Augustine's consolation when he preached to the boatmen of Hippo, and to the half-barbarous inhabitants of Cæsarea. In order to correct the people of Hippo for indulging too freely in their festivities he took the Holy Scriptures in his hand, read out the strongest rebukes he could find, and begged his audience, by the reproaches and sorrows of Jesus Christ, by His cross and blood, not to lose their souls through such excesses.

While he spoke to them, their tears forestalled his own, and he had the consolation of seeing these people docile and reformed. The inhabitants of Cæsarea were accustomed to celebrate public games, in which they attacked each other with indescribable fury, and pursued each other to death with drawn swords. St. Augustine undertook to dissuade them from this cruel custom. He spoke with such force and dignity that he excited their applause; but he began to hope for their conversion only when he saw their tears. "When I saw their tears flow," he said, "I believed that this horrible custom which they had received from their ancestors, and which had tyrannised over them for so long, would be abolished. It is now more than eight years since this people, by the grace of Jesus Christ, have attempted anything of the kind."

Twenty years ago, another Augustine, Monsignor Plantier, our illustrious predecessor, raised his voice against Bull-fights, which are a disgrace to our manners, and which make foreigners ask whether the town of Nismes is really a Christian city. Monsignor Plantier declared himself incapable of meeting this reproach, bowed his head and set himself resolutely to the task of abolishing this cruel custom and its tyranny over his flock.

We have heard those who quote this pastoral instruction, which gained him the applause of all France, say: "The Bishop has lost his time, public customs are stronger than eloquence, reason or even humanity. We must tolerate what we cannot either hinder or prevent. On this point Nismes will remain deaf to all the reproaches of its Bishops; do what you like, Nismes will continue to have its games."

They also say: "It is necessary to distinguish between games and fights. Our traditional games in these parts have nothing dangerous about them; the Spanish Bull-fights, on the contrary, merit severe censure. We use pads to deaden the sharpness of the animals' horns. Our agile Toreadors know how to avoid them at a bound, after having just roused them. Moreover, they are only bulls from Camangue which bear all the brunt of our games, their strength is not very great, they are easily appeased, and they rarely kill anybody."

By such excuses as these has the taste of the populace for these diversions been maintained. But moderation has come to be considered weakness, witnessing the games has given people a fancy for Bull-fights. The blood which was rarely shed has made them desire to see more, and after having begged to be allowed to witness the so-called innocent games, they now solicit sights which are full of horror. "Allow, tolerate, give free course to Bull-fights; public opinion demands such relaxation." No, we cannot grant the toleration asked for, we cannot take the course pointed out to us. We must speak in our turn, whether we are listened to or not, or rather, it is not we who speak, but the sight recently presented in our arenas. Since 20,000 persons had the pitiable temerity to indulge their eyes in gazing upon it, let them now open their ears to listen to the horrible description of it.

The Press got up the whole affair, and it is the Press which has made the most of the strange beauty of the scene. Advertisements, posters, hand-bills, descriptions, praises of the foreign troupe who crossed the Pyrenees on purpose to amuse the public, nothing was left undone. What thrilling pleasures! As if there could be any wholesome sense of enjoyment in seeing six bulls killed, sixteen horses expiring beneath their feet, and in the midst of this butchery, a Toreador, the most celebrated blade in Spain, risking his life amidst a number of beasts which were soon to be killed in a sea of blood. A glorious spectacle this, for a great city! Nor is this all. The Press, which favours Bull-fights, has its casuists. It has been asked, in several papers, whether, when a Toreador is killed, it is proper to leave the show.

KINDNESS TO ANIMALS.

Some have put the question, many have remained silent, and one paper has had the unfortunate audacity to publish an opinion intended to pursuade the crowd not to budge when confronted with homicide. Truly, what manners, what century have we gone back to? When Britannicus was poisoned by Nero, some of the guests fled, the rest were silent and watched the countenance of their master in order to compose their own, and, after a few moments' silence, the joys of the feast recommenced. Such is the impassiveness recommended by our casuists at the sight of bloodshed. They would steel men's hearts against pity, and this pity would seem to them shameful.

On the eve of the great day curiosity grows in excitement. A triumphal reception is given to the procession of bulls whose blood is about to flow in our arenas, of the horses to be ridden by the Matadors, and to the stranger who is about to offer himself to the applause or to the hisses of the public, according as his sword-thrusts enthral them by their skill, or disappoint them by their awkwardness.

The papers lavish the most flattering epithets on the troupe which parades the streets and squares. All will be great, splendid, sublime. No terms are pompous enough for raising to the rank of a great institution a spectacle worthy of pagan barbarism.

And it is to enjoy this that the neighbouring towns sent their citizens, that 20,000 spectators crowded our arenas to overflowing. The Magistrates presided at these public games; 80,000 francs were received. This money was paid in advance, and when one comes to think of this day so ardently longed for, all one can say is,

that money was lavishly spent to buy . . . to
buy what? The right of seeing these beasts
killed by a man who barely escaped the danger
of perishing with them.

Yes, six bulls were killed, and the programme
was carried out. Their flanks were pierced as
usual by sword-thrusts, they roared and foamed
with rage, they hurled themselves upon the
horses and trampled them under foot. They
overthrew and wounded the rider who attacked
them, they received gaping wounds, they groaned
forth their last gasp of dying fury in the
presence of 20,000 spectators, and rose to the
full height of the demands of a great Spanish
show. Let those who like this sort of thing
rejoice in it; we close our eyes at the thought of
this horrible scene, far as we are from it. For
them, they feast on it after having seen it, their
joy overflows, their eyes drink deep of it, their
hearts are swollen. Since the fights of 1863,
nothing like this has been seen in the Nismes
arenas. The fate of the horse was no happier
than that of the bull. We love this noble
animal, one of the best friends of man. He is
used for racing, but racing is not dangerous, and
he shares its glory with his rider. He is ridden
into battle, but he sheds his blood for the father-
land, and his wounds are hidden by victorious
laurels. Here nothing is noble, nothing great,
nothing useful. You cannot recognise the swift
horse bounding and stamping the earth with
his footmarks, and dashing headlong against
hosts of armed men. When the trumpet sounds,
he does not answer "Aha!" and, so far from
scenting the battle with gladness, he only smells
the shambles. Go, poor victim, into these

arenas dishonoured by shameful pleasure. Be a spectacle to the inquisitive crowd who have paid to see you gored to death. A bull's horn, not the sword's point, will fell you to the earth, and the hands which applauded you two months ago, when you won the prize at the racecourse, will be raised to clap and applaud when you breathe your last helplessly beneath the feet of a furious bull. Yesterday man was your friend; to-day he leaves you as an unworthy prey to your fate. Yesterday he vaunted your triumphs; to-day he celebrates your defeat and death. Five horses fell on August 9th in this unworthy combat, without honour and without glory.

Only the blood of man was wanting, and that blood was shed. The leader of the dance was carried out of the arena at the beginning of the fight, and the spectacle went on, notwithstanding the anxiety caused by his wounds. We must now look at the field of battle, these six bulls sacrificed for the pleasure of the lookers-on. Their fury only made the sight more horrible: then, besides the five horses killed on the spot, see these eleven others so soon to breathe their last; look, too, at the crowd so full of mingled feelings, sometimes applauding, sometimes whistling and groaning. Mothers left the scene that their children might not witness such revolting and tragic horrors. Public opinion is divided: some say they are satisfied, others seem undeceived, and if report is true, a party has been formed who are asking if it is not time to abolish these Bullfights. Ah, why do you hesitate to attend to the pressing entreaties of the Church, to the demands of humanity, and to the voice of your own real interest?

The Church, which has a horror of bloodshed, has condemned these spectacles ever since she has been able to raise her voice among the nations. Witness the Council of Carthage, which excommunicated those who, on holy days, deserted the Christian assemblies to attend public games. Tertullian, Salvian, Chrysostom, Augustine employed all their eloquence, and with tears of pity entreated Antioch, Rome, Carthage, and Marseilles to give up the dangerous pleasures of the circus and the amphitheatre. Listen to Pius V. addressing all the people on the earth by his bull dated November 1st, 1567. He declares that Bull-fights are not the work of men, but an invention of the devil; that they are opposed to Christian piety, to evangelical charity, and to the safety of the soul; and he says that those who frequent them deserve the censure of the Church. Spain protested against this severity, but three centuries of experience have made her wiser, and when our immortal predecessor lifted up his voice against this abominable custom, the Bishops of Spain were the first to congratulate and applaud him.

You are proud of moving with the age, and of partaking its generous sentiments and noble thoughts. Very well! This century has devoted much of its care and legislation to animals. The laws of France protect domestic animals against the brutality of man, and yet it is on the soil of France that they torture and wound and kill them at pleasure, without motive or excuse, merely at the request of pitiless amateurs, who use an unscrupulous Press to excite the curiosity of an unreasoning and thoughtless crowd. Exceptions are demanded for the corner of the world we live

in ; as if, because we are in the Province of
Languedoc, we did not belong to humanity.
People plead custom, as if custom should prevail
against duty, virtue, and law. They say that the
people of the South cannot do without these
sights, and yet near Nismes, where they have so
lately been displayed, Uzès, Alais, and Le Vigan,
the three principal towns of our Diocese, have
no taste for them. How is it that only three
leagues apart they are so indispensable to some,
and so indifferent to others? Does not the same
blood run in the veins of the people? Custom
tyrannises over one town and spares another.
It is not then so difficult to root it out and
abolish it. Oh, cruel customs! Why preserve
them when they amaze and scandalize the reason
of mankind?

They are unknown at Toulouse, Lyons,
Bordeaux, and Paris. Last year an attempt to
introduce these abominable games into Paris
was rejected with indignation and horror. The
legislators have condemned them, and I do not
know by what authority your magistrates have
been allowed to authorize and to defend what
ought to be everywhere forbidden, condemned,
and for ever cursed. Have politics anything to
do with it? We do not know; but we do know
and feel what humanity prescribes, and we
demand it with all the energy of reason, the tears
of pity, and with jealousy for our national honour.
Moreover, we will make ourselves the organ of
your best interests. When you are menaced with
the contagious illness which has decimated Spain,
and has attacked Marseilles with its mysterious
ravages, is it prudent and reasonable to assemble
under a burning sun, to brave a tropical heat,

to kindle a fire of feverish excitement in your veins by the sight of bloodshed? Calm and quiet living will enable you to avoid the plague, and you will take it by crowding together in the narrow precincts of a Bull-fight.

Not only is public health endangered, but foresight, domestic economy, and the care you owe to your family.

It is at the gates of these arenas that the workman spends his earnings, and the domestic servant his savings, the school-boy his little pleasures, the poor and the beggar the bread they get from public charity. What will become of them next day, after the short and evil pleasure they have enjoyed? Are you who are rich and live at ease more excusable? To-morrow we shall ask your gifts for our Holy Father the Pope, for the free schools, for our missions, for the great seminary. What will be your offering? Perhaps you will slip away from the annoyance of refusing and the obligation of giving; perhaps you will diminish your offerings just when they ought to be more abundant, for St. Peter's pence have become more necessary than ever. We are obliged to multiply our free schools under the pressure of persecution, the blood of martyrs flows in our Missions in the Far East, we must come to the assistance of these ravaged Christian communities; finally, our great seminary has no other resource than your charity, and the future of our priesthood is in your hands. Is it a time to spend money in the luxury, the pleasure, the cruelty of these pagan spectacles?

I hear it said publicly that you require these pleasures, and that the Sundays weary you. Ah! by all means give yourself pleasures which bring you repose and relaxation, and no heart will bless them more that the heart of your Bishop. These pure and Christian pleasures, who knows them better than you do? Who has less need of public games, arenas and amphitheatres? When we show strangers the villas, the pretty little houses, the verdure and the flowers, and, in the language of the country, the "Mazets," which abound on our hill sides, there, we say to them, is the sacred place which our Catholics of Nismes frequent on Sundays. The roof, brown with smoke, covers a small room where a humble and frugal repast is prepared. In front of it extends a lawn planted with almond trees, on which you will see both flowers and fruit, and olive trees which keep their sweet harvest until the end of autumn.

Thither our good Christian families repair in the evening for rest and fresh air. The mother looks after her household, the father reckons up the fruit on his little property, and the children race or play at ball under the eyes of their parents. You can meet them after vespers, carrying their meals on their arms, and taking the path to their little cottage. You will see them returning to the town after sunset, with serene faces and joyous steps, showing in their movements and their countenances the modest assurance of a quiet conscience. Then on the Monday the work of the week begins again, without weighing unduly on this humble household, because they have enjoyed the prayer and the liberty of Sunday, and because they have tasted the repose of their "Mazet" among the olive trees and fig trees which shade its walls. "Happy people," says the stranger, "may they long enjoy their happiness." Happy is the town that always keeps these simple customs, these Christian habits, and that never knows any paths but those which lead to the church, the workshop, the school, and the cottage in the fields!

I finish with these wishes so honourable to you, so consoling to me, and I pray God to spare us for ever the spectacle of a Bull-fight. May that of August 9th, 1883, be the last inflicted on the town of Nismes. May this pastoral instruction, which has cost so much to our heart and our pen, be the last reproach of your Bishops on this lamentable subject. May we have to congratulate ourselves that, through your wisdom, your repugnance, and your disgust, we have forced the promoters of these cruel amusements to seek applause and spectators elsewhere.

In this matter, and in the sacred name of God, we issue the following orders:—1st. We forbid all our people to attend Bull-fights, declaring, conformably to the bull of Pius V., that they will commit a grave error if they disobey our commands. 2nd. We condemn, unhesitatingly, the games which are given in some parishes; they are dangerous to both animals and men, they excite an unwholesome curiosity, they perpetuate bad habits, and if we do not go so far as to forbid them as sins, we earnestly desire to see the custom disappear from among us. The civil authority, which has so often attempted it, will do a true service to the Department of Gard, when it has the power to abolish them, and, above all, the courage to persevere in its decrees.

We have definitely forbidden the Catholic newspapers in our Diocese to publish advertisements or descriptions of Bull-fights. If they raise their voices it must be in loud condemnation of

KINDNESS TO ANIMALS.

them. It is no excuse to say that the advertisements are paid for ; this is not an excuse, but the aggravation of a fault. The Church is not honoured nor supported by public prints in which the account of a pilgrimage or the announcement of a musical Mass is interspersed with the praise of a theatre which she condemns, or of a combat which she abhors.

Pastoral Instruction and Proclamation of Monsignor Besson, Bishop of Nismes, on Bull Fights and Games.

Pastoral Works and Speeches of the Bishop of Nismes, Uzès, and Alais, 1883-1887. *Third Series.*

Pastoral Instruction and Proclamation on Bull Fights and Games, August 15*th,* 1885.

Animals in Saints' Lives and Legends.

He prayeth best who loveth best
 All things both great and small;
For the dear God who loveth us,
 He made and loveth all.

COLERIDGE.

Animals in Saints' Lives and Legends.

SAINT GAMELBERT,

Parish Priest in Bavaria about the Year 800.

SUCH was his kindness of heart, that he used to buy the little birds caught by the peasants, in order to set them free. He never allowed his servants to work in the fields or woods, if bad weather threatened. He valued, above everything, peace and concord, and kept the peace among his parishioners as far as he possibly could.

"*The Little Bollandists.*" *Lives of the Saints, by Monsignor Paul Guérin. Seventh Edition. Paris: Bloud and Barral*, 1882.

BLESSED ANDREW OF SEGNI.

A.D. 1302.

HE was very compassionate, and his general tenderness extended even to animals. One day he was ill, and his friends brought him some little birds, killed in shooting, in order to tempt him to eat, when the Saint felt sorry for the poor little creatures lying lifeless and bleeding before him. He made the sign of the cross over them, and prayed God to receive them. As soon as he had finished his prayer, the birds began to move, spread their wings, and flew away.

" The Little Bollandists."

THE BLESSED JORDAN OF SAXONY,

Dominican.

AMONG the men of God who have made the family of St. Dominic illustrious, we must not forget the blessed Jordan. Saxony considers it an honour to be his native country.

Not only men felt the charm God gave to the words of His servant. One day when some monks outwent St. Jordan in travelling just outside Lausanne, a weasel ran in front of them. The brethren gathered round the hole into which it had disappeared. The blessed Jordan, coming up, asked them, "Why are you stopping there?" They said: "Because a lovely, delightful little creature has gone into this hole." Then, bending down, he cried : "Come out, pretty little creature, that we may see you." The animal came at once to the mouth of the hole, and looked up at the saint, who made it get up into one of his hands, and stroked its head and back; it allowed him to do so. Then he said to it : "Now return to thy little home, and blessed be the Lord thy Creator." It at once obeyed and disappeared.

"The Little Bollandists."

SAINT WILLIAM FIRMATUS.

IT is said of him that even the wildest birds would approach him without fear, and come and eat out of his hand, and take refuge under his clothes from the cold. When he sat by a pond near his cell, the fish would swim to his feet and readily allow themselves to be taken up by the servant of God, who put them back into the water without hurting them.

One day his clerk came running to him, and told him that a wild boar was ravaging the garden, and destroying nearly all the vegetables.

William went to the fierce animal, and took it gently by the ear. The wild boar, as tame as a lamb, let itself be led by the saint into his cell ;

there it passed the night, and was only liberated early the next morning, after a kindly warning not again to destroy gardens belonging to its clergyman. It should be added that Saint William made the wild boar fast all night in his cell.

"*The Little Bollandists.*"

SAINT CUTHBERT, BISHOP OF LINDISFARNE.

According to F. Cashier, the swan is chiefly assigned to this saint, for this bird has been chosen as an emblem of men who are particularly attached to a solitary life, since it is generally very silent. However, we are inclined to think that the bird here mentioned was the downy goose, and not the swan.

Let us judge from what M. de Montalembert says:—"They used to swarm on the rock (of Lindisfarne) in former days, and are still found there, though in much smaller numbers, on account of the people who come and steal their nests and shoot them. These birds were found nowhere else in the British Isles, and were called the birds of St. Cuthbert. It is he who, according to a monk of the thirteenth century, inspired their hereditary confidence because he took them for companions of his solitude, and was careful that no one should disturb them in their habits."

"*The Little Bollandists.*"

SAINT MARSUS, MONK OF AUXERRE.

A.D. 462.

WITH the remembrance of St. Mamertinus, one associates that of St. Marsus, his disciple. Marsus had quitted the country of the Bituriges on account of the persecution inflicted on Catholics by the Arian Goths, who were then in possession of it. Received into the Monastery of Auxerre by Mamertinus, he fulfilled the humble duties of shepherd and cowherd in the stables and farms of the monks, and sanctified himself in the performance of them. His story is full of miracles. He used to call the little birds to him and feed them, and, by his word of command, he sent away the bears and other animals which are hostile to man and his flocks.

"*The Little Bollandists.*"

SAINT FRUCTUOSUS, ARCHBISHOP OF BRAGA.

One day he was going through a forest, when a roe, pursued by hunters, took refuge under his cloak. The Saint took the animal under his protection, and brought it to the monastery. The grateful beast never quitted his liberator; it followed him about all day, slept at his feet at night, and never ceased to cry when he was absent. More than once he had it taken back to the forest, but it always found the track of its deliverer's footprints. At last it was one day killed by a young man who disliked monks. Fructuosus was absent for a few days, and on his return he was surprised not to see his roe run to meet him, and when he heard that it was dead, he was overcome with grief, his knees trembled, and he prostrated himself on the floor of the church. It is not related whether this was to ask God to punish the cruel man; but the latter soon fell ill, and sent for the Father to come to his assistance. Fructuosus took the revenge of a noble Visigoth and Christian. He cured the murderer of his roe, and restored him to health both of soul and body.

It is related of him that, wishing to escape the homage of the people, he retired into the depth of the forest, and that the jays which he had brought up in the monastery sought him out and betrayed the place of his retreat by the joyous chattering with which they greeted him. Fructuosus is painted with a roe and jays as his emblems.

"*The Little Bollandists.*"

SAINT MARCULPH,

First Abbot of Nanteuil in the Diocese of Coutances.

As he was making his second journey to the court to obtain the confirmation of the donations made to his monasteries, he rested on the banks of the Vise. A hare, pressed hard by the hounds, took refuge under his habit, but the hunters compelling the Saint to let it go, the poor animal ran away, while the horses and hounds remained immovable.

"*The Little Bollandists.*"

SAINT GODRIC,

Pedlar and Hermit in England.

ONE day there was a grand hunt near Godric's hermitage. A magnificent stag was chased by the relations of Bishop Ramulf. The poor creature came panting to Godric's cell, as if asking for refuge.

Godric, on emerging from his retreat, saw it trembling with fear, and seeming to implore his help. Godric, indeed, took it into his cell, and the noble animal lay down at his feet. The hunters, however, soon came up and demanded their prey. Godric went to meet them. They asked him where the stag was. He answered, "God knows."

The hunters, recognising beneath the rags of the poor hermit an angel and a Saint, went away with their hounds without disturbing Godric or the stag any more, and the latter, to get over its fright, passed the night in the hermitage. The next morning it returned joyfully into the forest, and it came back several times a year to express its gratitude by caresses.

Godric became the natural protector of the beasts in the forest pursued by the hunters: hares, deer, etc., when in danger, fled to him for safety. During the cold of winter the little birds warmed themselves in his breast; one would have said that they recognised in him the son of their merciful Creator.

The hermit-pilgrim, St. Godric, is often painted surrounded by serpents, because dangerous animals came to him without hurting him.

"*The Little Bollandists.*"

SAINT AVENTINE,

Apostle of Gascony, and Martyr, A.D. 538.

ONE day, according to his custom, Aventine quitted his cell and betook himself to a grove overlooking the vale of Aosta, that he might pray there quietly amidst its mysterious shade. On his knees, with uplifted eyes and glowing heart, he blessed God whom he inwardly adored. A very deep silence favoured his recollection, and his happy soul seemed to be as serene as paradise. Suddenly the silence was broken by the plaintive roar of a bear which was laboriously coming down from the mountains. Aventine saw it, but was not alarmed; he knew that He who watched over Daniel in the den of lions would also watch over him. It was not the wild animals of the forest that were to shed his blood—this blood was reserved to gratify the rage of human persecutors far more savage than they. As if led by an invisible hand or by some kindly instinct the wounded animal came straight to him as quietly as a lamb, and lifted its heavy paw in which was a long thorn, and laid it quite confidingly in the hands of Aventine, as if imploring help.

The servant of God kindly examined the wound and extracted the cruel thorn, and then the grateful bear left him after loading him with caresses.

This fact, which we have taken from the chronicle, is not without a certain authority. There still exists in a parish of the valley, and not far from the hermitage of St. Aventine, another ruin, a precious remnant of the little oratory raised by the faithful to preserve the memory of this remarkable event. Tradition persistently reports that it is here that the Saint met the bear. A wood carving on the reredos of the church of St. Aventine recalls this circumstance in the life of the Saint, and the old woodwork showed a similar incident. A bear was seen standing before the Saint, who was taking the thorn out of its paw with a pointed instrument.

" The Little Bollandists."

BLESSED MARTIN OF PERRES,

Monk of the Third Order of St. Dominic.

IT made him very unhappy to see foundlings and young orphans exposed to all sorts of hardships. In order to obviate this sad circumstance he had built a celebrated college at Lima, where they could be brought up in piety and taught to lead honest lives. His goodness was so great that he did not except animals from his kindness, and he often gave them his skilful help and care. It pleased God to honour by His celestial favours the noble charity of His servant.

Nearly all Spanish America calls him the *Rats' Saint*, because they say that his picture, if placed in the haunts of rats and mice, speedily causes these animals to disappear. In his convent in Peru the sacristan complained that the rats gnawed away his things, and proposed to destroy the disagreeable visitors with poison. Brother Martin dissuaded him from this cruelty. He then called all these little creatures and put a basket which he was holding upon the ground, and when they had all scrambled into the basket he carried them into the garden, promising to look to them every day, if they would cease from ravaging the provisions of the monastery. This is why he is represented with a basket in his hand surrounded by rats, either that he is about to feed them or to take them from the sacristy and gather them in the garden, in order to supply them with the leavings of the house. The Blessed Martin of Perrés is the patron of coloured people, and he is invoked against rats.

" The Little Bollandists."

ST. COLUMBAN AND OTHERS.

The rival of St. Benedict, St. Columban, was born the same year in which the Patriarch of Monte Cassino died. He frequently left his disciples to bury himself in the woods, and live in community with the animals.

There, as afterwards, in his long and intimate communion with the rough and wild nature of these lonely places, nothing alarmed him, and nothing was afraid of him. Everything obeyed his voice. The birds came to him to be petted, and the squirrels ran down from the tops of the firs to hide themselves in the folds of his cowl. St. Columban is painted blessing wild animals.

WHILST the chiefs and retainers of the French aristocracy only came occasionally into the forest gloom, and that merely for the pleasure of destruction, where the monks spent the whole of their lives, the religious naturally dwelt in a sort of familiarity with most of the wild animals which they saw romping around them, and they had leisure to observe their instincts and habits, and were easily able to tame them. It seemed as if they respected each other by a sort of instinctive pact. Among the innumerable legends describing religious life in the heart of the forest, we cannot find any record of a monk's being devoured, or even threatened by any of the most ferocious animals ; neither do we find that the monks ever hunted, even when tempted to do so by the pangs of hunger, to which, in its extremest forms, they were very often exposed.

How, then, can we wonder that the game, on being hunted and wounded by merciless strangers, sought refuge with the peaceable guests of the solitude which they shared ? And, above all, how easy it is to understand that Christian populations, accustomed for centuries to find among the monks help and protection from every kind of violence, soon learnt to record with pleasure the touching legends which consecrated under a poetic and popular form the thought that the dwelling-places of the Saints were an inviolable refuge for weakness from every form of violence.

One of the first and most curious examples of these relations between kings and monks, in which the beasts of the forests acted as intermediaries, is that of Childebert and holy Abbot Karilef. Whilst cultivating an out-of-the-way corner of the earth, the Saint lived surrounded by all kinds of animals, and, among others, by a wild buffalo, of a very rare kind in that country, which he had succeeded in completely taming. The legend says that it was delightful to see the venerable old man standing by the side

of the monster stroking it, and rubbing it gently
between the horns or along the great dewlap and
the fleshy folds of its thick neck, after which
the grateful animal, still true to its instinct,
galloped away to the depths of the forest.

Childebert, son of Clovis, is the great hero of
monastic legends. Having arrived at the Maine,
accompanied by Queen Ultrogoth, in order to
devote himself to ordinary amusement, he learnt
with pleasure that a buffalo, an animal already
very rare, and almost unknown in Gaul, had
been seen in those parts. Everything was arranged
for the fullest success of the next day's hunting.
The buffalo, frightened out of its wits, took
refuge in his friend's cell, and when the huntsmen
arrived they saw the man of God standing before
the animal to protect it.

On the shores of the Mediterranean, a Greek
of noble birth, named Ægidius, had in his youth
followed the footsteps of Lazarus and of the
Magdalen, and landed at the mouth of the Rhône
where he grew old in solitude in the depths of a
vast forest, having no other nourishment than the
milk of a hind which came to rest in his grotto.
One day, as the king of the country, whose name
was, according to some, Childeberg, King of the
Franks, and, according to others, Flavin, King
of the Goths, was hunting in the forest, the hind
was found, and was chased by the huntsmen
into the cavern. One of them shot an arrow at
it, and pierced the recluse's hand stretched out to
protect it.

A similar feature is found in the legend of St.
Nennoca, the young and beautiful daughter of

a Breton king, who had refused the man her father wished her to marry, in order that she might go to Armorica and lead a religious life. The Prince of that country, being in pursuit of a stag near the monastery, saw the animal, half dead with fatigue, take refuge within the sacred precincts, while the hounds stopped short without venturing to follow. Alighting from his horse, and entering the church, he found the stag lying at the feet of the young Abbess, in the midst of the choir of nuns who were chanting the Office.

After King Clotaire II. had succeeded to the Frankish monarchy he once went to hunt in the forest domains of Sequania, and pursued an immense wild boar into an oratory inhabited by an old Irish monk, Descoles, who had come to Gaul with St. Columban. He was so touched at seeing this ferocious animal lying before the little altar, before which the foreign recluse was praying, that he presented the latter with everything in the cell which belonged to the royal treasury. The donation was accepted, and the man of God, after saving the life of the wild boar, took care to have it set free, and to assure its flight to the depths of the forest. The great nobles, who were as fond of the chase and as assiduous therein as the kings themselves, were like them subject to the influence of the monks, when the latter appealed to them for protection of the guests of their solitude. Basolus, born of a noble family in Limousin, and founder of the monastery of Viergy on the mountain of Reims, had built a cell in the thickest part of the forest, under the shelter of a stone cross; his only furniture was a small desk, beautifully carved, whereon to rest the Holy Scriptures, on which he continually meditated. One day he was disturbed in his prayers by an enormous wild boar, which threw itself at his feet as if to beg for its life. Following the animal on horseback came one of the most powerful nobles of the neighbourhood, named Atlila, whom the mere look of the Saint stopped dead and kept immovable. He was really a good man, says the legend, though he was a mighty hunter. He proved it by giving to the Abbot all the land he possessed round his cell. Four centuries later the remembrance of this remained so vivid, that, by a convention scrupulously observed, all game hunted in the forest of Reims, if it could get to the little wood overlooked by the cross of St. Basolus, was spared by the hounds and the huntsmen.

In the same way as his famous brethren in the East, the Patriarch of the Western Monks had his tame bird, only it came to ask nourishment from him instead of bringing it to him. St. Gregory the Great, in his biography of the Saint, says that in his first monastery at Subiaco, St. Benedict saw at each of his meals a raven come from the forest, so that he fed it from his hand.

These anecdotes, piously transmitted by the greatest lights of the Church, prepare us to listen without surprise to many other accounts of the friendship between the monks and animals.

Sometimes it is the wild sparrows that fly down from the top of the trees to pick the grains of corn or crumbs of bread from the hand of that Abbot Maxentius before whom Clovis knelt on his return from his victory over Alaric ; and thus the people found out how great was his gentleness and mildness. Sometimes it is other little birds which come to seek their food and to be caressed by Waleric, whom we shall very soon see as one of the most illustrious disciples of St. Columban, the apostle of Ponthieu and the founder of the great monastery of Leuconnaiis. Charmed with their gentle company, when his disciples drew near him, and the larks flew round him in much alarm, he stopped the monks and beckoned them to retire. "My sons," said he, "do not let us frighten my little friends, nor do them any harm ; let them take their fill of what we have left." Again, it is Karilef who, while dressing and pruning the little vine, the poor fruit of which he had offered to King Childebert, overcome by heat and fatigue, takes off his monk's frock and hangs it up in an oak ; and then, at the end of his hard day's work, on going to put on his garment, finds that a wren, the smallest and most inquisitive of our birds, has made a nest in it and laid an egg there. The holy man was so filled with delight and admiration that he passed all the night in giving thanks to God.

An exactly similar trait is told of Saint Malo, one of the great monastic apostles who have left their names to the dioceses to the north of Armorica. The only difference is that this Saint allowed the bird to nest in his cloak until the little ones were hatched out.

Naturally the wild animals sought out and preferred to remain in the lands possessed by such kind and gentle masters, and thence arose the amusing little story of St. Magloire and Count Loïescon. This very rich Armorican noble, whom Magloire had cured of leprosy, made the monk a present of half of a large domain, washed by the sea. When Magloire went to take possession of it, all the birds in the forest and the fishes in the sea rushed to the part given to the Saint, as if they wished to have him only as master. When the Count and his wife saw the half of their domain thus depopulated, they were very sorry, and insisted on Magloire exchanging his half for theirs. No sooner was this done than the birds and the fishes followed Magloire, going and coming so as to be always where the monks were.

From Montalembert's "Monks of the West." Paris: Victor Lecoffre.

SAINT COLUMBA,

Apostle of Caledonia, 521-597.

His patriotic melancholy never left him, and later on in life we see it reappear in a circumstance in which we find his constant regret for his loss of Ireland side by side with a tender and watchful solicitude for all God's creatures. One morning he called a monk of Iona and said to him, "Go and sit by the sea, on the strand to the west of this island; there you will see a poor wandering stork arrive from the north of Ireland. It will have been for a long time buffeted by the winds, and it will fall at your feet exhausted on the shore. You must take it up tenderly and care for it and feed it for three days; after it has had three days' rest, when it has revived and quite recovered its strength, it will not wish to prolong its exile among us, it will fly back to sweet Ireland, its dear country where it was born. I recommend it thus to your care because it comes from my own native land."

All happened as the Saint had foreseen and ordered. The evening of the day on which the monk had received the traveller, and when he returned to the monastery, Columba asked him no questions, but said to him: "God bless you dear son, who have taken care of the exile; in three days you will see it return to its country." And, in fact, at the appointed time the stork rose in the air before the eyes of its host and, after looking about a while for its route, flew across the sea straight to Ireland. The sailors of the Hebrides all know and tell this story. I hope there are none of my readers who would not repeat and merit the blessing of Columba.

Leaving the cell to return to the monastery, he sat down about half way thither, at a place still marked by one of the ancient crosses of Iona. Just at this moment he saw an old and faithful servant, that is to say, the old white horse which was employed to bring the milk from the farm for the daily sustenance of the monks, run up to him. It came and laid its head on his master's shoulder as if to take leave of him. The eyes of the old horse had such a plaintive expression that they seemed to be full of tears. Diarmid wished to drive it away, but the good old man prevented him. "This horse loves me; let him too mourn my departure. The Creator has revealed to him what He has hidden from thee, a man endowed with reason." After this he caressed the animal and gave him a parting benediction.

Montalembert's "Monks of the West."

SAINT FRANCIS OF ASSISI.

HE sometimes passed hours in praising the industry of bees; and he, who had nothing for himself, used to feed them in winter with honey and wine, so that they should not die of cold. He proposed as models for his disciples the diligence of larks and the innocence of doves. Still, nothing equalled his love of lambs, which recalled to him the humility and tenderness of the Saviour. It is said that, when travelling with a monk in the March of Ancona, he met a man carrying two little lambs hung over his shoulder by a cord. When the Blessed Francis heard their bleating he was filled with pity, and drew near and said to the man, "My brother, why do you torture the lambs by carrying them thus bound and hung up?" The man answered that, being pressed for money, he was taking them to a neighbouring market to sell them to the butchers, who would kill them. "God forbid," cried the saint. "Rather take the cloak I am wearing and give me the lambs." The man was only too pleased to give up the lambs and take the cloak in exchange, which was much more valuable, and had been lent to the Saint that morning by a faithful Christian on account of the coldness of the weather.

St. Francis, however, held the lambs in his arms, but did not know what to do with them. After consulting with his companion he restored them to their first master, making him promise faithfully never to sell them nor do them any harm, but to take great care of them and nourish them well. Everything in this tale is charming, and one does not know which to admire most, the tenderness of the Saint for the little lambs, or his guileless confidence in their master.

St. Francis, by his innocence and simplicity, had, one might almost say, returned to the condition of Adam, when our first father saw all the animals in a divine light, and loved them with a fraternal charity. Animals, on their side, were as obedient to him as to the first man, and for him returned to the conditions which sin has destroyed. It is a common and noteworthy trait in many saints that these regenerate souls have resumed the ancient power of man over nature. The Fathers of the Thebaid were served by ravens and lions; St. Gall commanded the Alpine bears. When St. Columban traversed the forest of Luxeuil, the birds came to play with him when he called them, and the squirrels ran down from the trees and sat on his hand. The life of St. Francis is full of similar facts, attested by eye-witnesses, which must be admitted, whether we explain them by the power of love, which sooner or later commands and obtains love, or whether in the presence of the servants of God the animals do not feel that instinctive horror with which our corruption and hardness inspire them. When the penitent of Assisi, worn out with fastings and watchings, left his cell and showed himself in the country parts of Umbria, it seems that in his emaciated features on which was so little left of this world, the animals saw only the Divine impress, and they came to him to admire and serve him. Hares and pheasants took refuge in the folds of his dress. If he passed a meadow, and, as his custom was, called the sheep as his sisters, it is said that they raised their heads and ran after him, leaving the shepherds astounded. He himself, so long separated from the joys of life, took a gentle pleasure in these entertainments prepared for him by the beasts of the field. One day, when he had ascended the mountain of Alvernia to pray, a great number of birds surrounded him with joyous cries, and flapped their wings as if to congratulate him on his arrival. Then the Saint said to his companion, "I see that it is the Divine will that we remain here a little while, because our little brothers the birds seem so consoled by our presence." When he began his course of preaching, it happened that as he was crossing the valley of Spoleto, not far from Bevagna, he passed a place where there were a great number of birds, and above all, of sparrows, rooks and doves. Observing this, the blessed servant of God, on account of the love he had for creatures devoid of reason, ran to the place, leaving his companions for a short time. As he drew near he saw that the birds were waiting for him, and he greeted them as was his wont. Then, wondering at them for not being alarmed at the sight of him, he was delighted, and begged them to listen to the Word of God. He said to them : " My brothers, little birds, you ought to be most grateful to your Creator and love Him always, because He has given you feathers to cover you, wings to fly with, and all that you need. He has made you noble among the works of His hands, and has chosen you your dwelling in the pure air, and without your having to sow or reap, He nourishes and governs you without allowing you to worry at all."

At these words, according to his own account and that of his companions, the birds drew themselves up and began to beat their wings. He, passing through the midst of them, went backwards and forwards, brushing them with his cloak. Then blessing them and making the sign of the cross over them, he let them fly away. After this, the blessed Father, full of consolation, went on with his companions. But as he was quite simple, not by nature but by grace, he began to accuse himself of negligence for not having preached to the birds before, since they listened with such respect to the Word of God.

There could not be a grander example than his horror of destruction, carried even to clearing the worms on the road out of the way, and to saving sheep from the butcher; this, too, in the century which supported the cruelties of Frederick II., and of his lieutenant Ezzelino the Ferocious, and which was also to see the torture of Ugolino, and the Sicilian Vespers. This man, who was simple enough to preach to flowers and birds, also evangelised the Guelf and Ghibelline towns: he assembled the citizens in the public squares of Padua, Brescia, Cremona, and Bologna, and began his discourse by wishing them peace. Then he exhorted them to extinguish enmities and to conclude treaties of reconciliation. And according to the witness of the chronicles of that time, many of those who had hated peace now began to love one another and to detest bloodshed.

It is thus that St. Francis of Assisi appeared as the Orpheus of the Middle Ages, calming the ferocity of beasts and the cruelty of man. It is nothing to be wondered at, that his voice should touch the wolves of the Apennines, if it could disarm the vengeance of Italians, whose wont it is never to pardon an enemy.

"*The Franciscan Poets in Italy in the Thirteenth Century*," by *A. F. Ozanam. Sixth Edition. Paris: Victor Lecoffre.* 1882.

Going back, says St. Bonaventura, to the origin of all things, Francis considered created beings as coming from the paternal heart of God. This community of origin made him feel a real fraternity between them all. "They have the same source as we have," he said. "Like us, they get the life of thought, will, and love from the Creator." He accepted to the letter what seemed to him the consequence of this truth.

Is it necessary to say how this conviction made him look on animals? He would not have hurt the smallest of them, and would not allow any one else to do so. "Oh! simple piety!" says Celano, "O loving symplicity! He would not crush a worm in his path, but carefully put it on one side, lest it should be trodden on by someone less careful than he."

Not to hurt our humble brethren, this he held was our first duty towards them; but to stop there, a complete misapprehension of the intentions of Providence. We have a higher mission. God wishes that we should succour them whenever they require it. The servant of Jesus Christ was very careful not to go against this Providential dispensation.

All creatures in distress had equal right to his protection. One day, on the road to Siena, he met a young man carrying live turtle doves, which he had taken, and was going to sell. "Oh, good young man," he said to him, "these innocent birds are compared in Holy Scripture to chaste and faithful souls. I earnestly beg you not to put them into the hands of those who will kill them, but to give them to me." They were given to him. The blessed Saint put them in his bosom, and said to them, while caressing them, "Oh! my doves—simple, innocent, and chaste—why do you let yourselves be caught? Now, I wish to save you from death and make you nests, so that you may have young ones, and multiply, according to the commands of the Creator." St. Francis was in for it, and made nests for all of them; and they became tame, and began to lay eggs, and hatch them in the presence of the brothers, as if they had always been hand-fed fowls. They did not go away until St. Francis gave them his blessing and allowed them to do so.

These rescues were necessarily rare. What happened daily was the care he showed to animals. He loved to see them all. The sight of them gave him pleasure. He was proud of their good qualities. He sought these good qualities in their innermost being, which he fathomed by special illuminations such as are given the blessed, as Celano says; and, when he discovered them, he praised them as he would have done those of a brother or sister. He was not afraid of spending a whole day in praising them. A hare and a tench, which were offered as presents to the Saint, could scarcly be persuaded to leave him. The same thing happened with a wild rabbit from an island in Lake Thrasymene. The rabbit followed his steps, and would not depart until the Saint had given it his benediction. More ceremony was required for a pheasant which a noble of the province of Siena had given him. The giver wished that he should eat it, in order to increase his strength, which declined daily; but to nourish himself was the last thought of St. Francis. He received the beautiful bird with extreme courtesy. "Brother pheasant," he said, "praise to our Creator!" The pheasant flapped its wings at this invitation. "We must see," said St. Francis, "whether our brother wishes to remain with us or to return to his woods." By his orders the bird was carried to a vineyard, but it flew back at once. They carried it still further off, but it returned before its bearer. It even entered the cell of St. Francis, slipping under the tunic of the brothers who guarded the entrance. For the time being, St. Francis embraced the faithful creature, and spoke caressingly to it, and ordered that something should be given it to eat. He did not, however, intend to keep it. He gave it to his doctor, who, having heard what had happened, was full of admiration, and begged to have it. But the pheasant was not of this way of thinking. At the house of the doctor it would not eat anything. They brought it back to the convent. It gazed at the Father for some time, and gave signs of the greatest joy, and began to eat with relish. "There is in all these traits such *naïve* and exquisite tenderness that one is tempted to smile and weep at the same time."

"*Histoire de S. François d'Assise.*" Par *l'Abbé Le Monier. Vol. II. Paris: Victor Lecoffre*, 1889.

We who were contemporaries of the blessed Francis and wrote this, are witnesses that we often heard him say: "When I speak to the Emperor I shall beg and entreat him, for the love of God and me, to make a special law that no man capture or kill his sisters the larks, or do them any injury. Also that all authorities of states, or lords of camps or manors, yearly on Christmas Day be commanded to oblige men to strew corn and other grains over the roads about their states and camps, that their sisters the larks and also other birds may have something to eat on so solemn a day, and that, out of reverence for the Son of God, whom the blessed Virgin laid between the ox and the ass in the manger, whosoever possesses ox or ass should be forced to make the best provision for them out of his stores on that night; in like manner that on such a day all the poor ought to be well filled with good food by the rich."

For the blessed Francis had greater respect for Christmas than for other festivals, and he said: "Since the Lord was born for us we ought to be saved." Wherefore he wished every Christian on that day to rejoice in the Lord, and out of love for Him Who gave Himself for us, that all should make liberal provision, not only for the poor, but for animals also and birds.

"Mirror of Perfection." Translated by Lady de la Warr. Burns & Oates.

ST. ANTONY OF PADUA PREACHING TO THE FISHES.
(*Gerard David.*) See p. 49.

SAINT ANTHONY OF PADUA.

Close to the Convent of Montpellier was a pool of water swarming with frogs, whose croaking greatly disturbed the recollection of the Brethren. Anthony commanded them to be silent, and they were as obedient to his orders as the birds on the shores of the Adriatic were to Saint Francis.

Azevedo. "Life of the Portuguese Wonder-Worker."

Manichæism, which had opened the floodgates of unbridled licence, had crept across the whole country. There were the Cathari in the Romagna, the Patari in the Milanese district, and the Waldenses in Sardinia. They were, one and all, violently opposed both to the Church and the State. . . . . In vain Anthony invited them courteously to meet him in argument; to all his advances they opposed a cold resistance or contempt and ridicule. . . . Making a sign to the people to follow him to the beach, he took his way to the mouth of the Marecchia, and then turning towards the wide expanse of the Adratic, he cried in a loud voice: "Ye fishes of the rivers, ye fishes of the sea, listen unto me. It is to you I have come to announce the Word of God, since men have turned away from Him, and refuse to listen." At the sound of his voice the waters became agitated. Shoal upon shoal of fishes, great and small, ploughed through the waves in eager haste, and arranged themselves in order along the shore, as far as the eye could reach, the smaller ones in front, the larger further back, all with their heads turned towards him who called them. Then he preached to them in these words:

"My brothers the fishes, you owe your Creator a vast debt of gratitude. It is He who has assigned to you for your abode this noble element, with its boundless expanse, wherein you may roam at large. It is He who has given you the shelter of the deep against the fury of the tempest; who has endowed you with strength and agility to glide swiftly through the waves, and who supplies you day by day with abundant food. When he created you he blessed you, and bade you increase and multiply. When He destroyed men and living creatures on the earth by the waters of the Deluge, He left you unmolested. It was upon you He conferred the privilege of saving the prophet Jonas; of furnishing the tribute money for the Word Incarnate, and of yielding Him nourishment both before and after His Resurrection. Bless, then, and praise the Lord, your Creator and Preserver, who has thus specially favoured you amongst His creatures."

The fishes, as though gifted with intelligence, testified by their movements the pleasure they took in listening to the Saints' words, and their readiness to render to the Most High the tribute of their mute homage.

"*St. Anthony of Padua.*" *By Father Léopold de Chérancé, O.S.F.C. Rendered into English by Father Marianus, O.S.F.C. Burns & Oates.*

SAINT PHILIP NERI.

Philip was very tender towards brute animals. Seeing someone put his foot on a lizard, he cried out; "Cruel fellow; what has that poor animal done to you?" Seeing a butcher wound a dog with one of his knives, he could not contain himself, and had great difficulty in keeping himself cool. He could not bear the slightest cruelty to be shown to animals under any pretext whatever. If a bird came into the room, he would have the window opened that it might not be caught.

PRAYER TO ST. PHILIP.

By Cardinal Newman.

Philip, my glorious Advocate, teach me to look at all I see around me after thy pattern as the creatures of God. Let me never forget that the same God who made me, made the whole world, and all men and animals that live in it. Gain me the grace to love all God's works for God's sake, and all men for the sake of my Lord and Saviour, who has redeemed them by the Cross. And especially let me be tender and compassionate and loving towards all Christians, as my brethren in grace. And do thou, who on earth wast so tender to all, be especially tender to us, and feel for us, hear us in all our troubles, and gain for us from God, with whom thou dwellest in beatific light, all the aids necessary for bringing us safely to Him and to thee.

"*Meditations and Devotions of the late Cardinal Newman.*" London: Longmans, Green and Co., 1893.

ONCE a little bird being found in the chapel where St. Philip was saying mass, he said to the man who held it in his hand: "Do not do it any harm, but let it go free." The bird took wing, and flew away; but the Saint said, as if he repented, sorrowfully: "Now I doubt whether the poor little thing will be able to find its supper."

"*The Compassion and Affection of S. Philip Neri for Animals.*" By Cardinal Capecelatro.

A LEGEND ABOUT OUR LORD.

"AND He was in the desert forty days and forty nights; and He was tempted by Satan, and He was with beasts, and the Angels ministered to Him" (Mark i. 13). A touching legend shows us the gracious Saviour, seated on a rock, with savage animals lying peacefully at His feet, and little birds singing sweet songs about His head, as they nestle in the folds of His garments. I learn from the sight of Jesus dwelling amongst animals, that purity and innocence attract all hearts, and that if I would resemble Jesus, I must live at peace with all, supporting the defects and ill-humour of my fellow creatures with patience and charity, showing kindness to those who are rough and overbearing, as well as to the meek and gentle. I learn also to be kind to all dumb animals, which are creatures of Jesus and which He loves—since He dwells amongst them, and I learn never wilfully to hurt them—but to cherish them, as each represents a thought of the Creator and a gift at His hands.

"*The most beautiful among the Children of Men : Meditations upon the life of our Lord Jesus Christ,*" *by Mrs. Abel Ram. Washbourne.* 1877.

ABBOT TOSTI, O.S.B.

On St. Benedict's Raven.

AND here we must make some remarks about the raven which was accustomed to come every day at a particular time to eat out of St. Benedict's hand. This fact may awaken in the mind of the reader an unworthy suspicion that the Saint wasted his time in taming ravens and other creatures. Men like St. Benedict, always contemplating the love of God the Creator, could not help loving all the works of His creation. In this way they felt themselves drawn by fraternal love to all things created by their common Father.

And besides this, animals without reason often by Divine ordinance lent themselves to the service of holy men, who, far from human companionship and in desert places, committed their lives to the hand of God. And, therefore, though alone and unharmed, they were never killed by the attacks of wild beasts. And thus we find in the lives of the Fathers in the desert, the raven bringing bread to St. Paul, the first hermit, and the two lions which came from the ends of the desert to dig the grave in which Antony placed his body. This diffusion of love, even to animals supposed not to have reason, made St. Francis call birds his brethren and even the wolf his brother.

From the " Life of St. Benedict."

SAINT ISIDORE,

Husbandman, Patron of Madrid.

WHEN he (Isidore) went into the field to his work, he not only distributed to the poor some of the wheat which he had taken with him to sow, but also gave some handfuls to the birds, saying, "Take, birds of God—that which God gives, He gives for all." The wheat-seed was diminished by this; but, miraculously, when he arrived at the farm, not a grain was wanting, and his baskets were as full as when he left home. The holy man recognised the miracle; he was confused, but not alarmed; he was silent and thankful, and with renewed confidence, when he again began to sow his seed, he said, "In the name of God, this is for God, this is for us, and this is for the birds, and this is for the ants." The labourers surrounding him heard this, and questioned as to why he said, "And this is for the ants." On this the Saint, thinking about the late miracle, answered simply, "It is: for God gives to all."

Being one day at the door of his house, he saw a hare pursued by greyhounds. The hare, very tired, went towards the farm; the Saint, with great compassion, said, "Greyhound, in the name of God I pray you have pity on the poor little thing, and do it no harm." A wonderful thing followed: the greyhound stopped at once, and the hare, being free, went at once to its lair.

"*Santos de la Imperial Ciudad de Toledo, y S. V. Arcobispado.*" *E. L. P. Antonio de Guintandueñas, S.J.*

SAINT FRANCIS DE SALES.

THE Church recommends to the clergy perfect gentleness. For this reason, ecclesiastics do not mix in affairs where blood is shed; and blood, even if justly shed, is one of the causes of irregularity. Our blessed Father excelled especially in gentleness: "And on account of his meekness he was led by the right hand of the Most High." The priests of the old dipensation had almost always something to do with blood, because of the sacrifices; and the law of Moses was so severe that one might say the same of it as was said of Draco's laws, that they were written in blood.

The laws of the new dispensation are not like this. Some have maintained that hunting was forbidden to the clergy, not only as unfitted by its nature and from the violent excitement of such an occupation, but because it ends in the death and blood of the animals pursued—so that they might learn to avoid all appearance of cruelty.

"Alas!" says St. Francis of Sales in reference to hunting, "what an infernal pleasure! It is thus that infuriated demons pursue poor souls with temptations and sins, that they may cast them into eternal death—and no one thinks of it."

This brings to my remembrance what he himself wrote about St. Anselm in his *Philothea*. Here are the words: "It is said that St. Anselm, Archbishop of Canterbury (whose birth greatly honours our mountains), was admirable in carry-

KINDNESS TO ANIMALS. 57

ing out good ideas. A hare, hard pressed by hounds, and in sore fear of death, took refuge under the holy prelate's horse as he was travelling along; the hounds gave tongue all ronnd, but dared not violate the shelter to which their prey had betaken itself. It was a curious thing, at which the train of hunters laughed, whilst the great Anselm wept, and, sighing, said, 'Ha! you laugh, but the poor animal does not. The enemies of the soul, when she has been driven and harassed by various contrivances into all kinds of sins, lie in wait in order to ravish and devour her. In her alarm, she seeks refuge in all directions; and, if she cannot find it, her enemies jeer and laugh.' Having said this, he went away, with a sigh." It is possible, my sisters, that this age, which deems itself strong-minded, may look upon these remarks as feeble; yet not only do the Scriptures not disdain to speak of Samson's foxes, of Balaam's ass, of Tobias's dog, but we read of St. John's partridge and St. Giles's hind; and many similar examples in the lives of the Saints show well enough that one may draw such examples from their teaching. But to you I need not excuse myself, because I know that these simple tales will greatly edify you.

While speaking of this, I am reminded of what St. Chrysostom said, wishing that someone could have remarked the least and most homely actions of St. Paul and the other Apostles; he thought they might have done much good as a rule of life to Christians in similar circumstances. I could wish that someone had described how St. Paul made his tents, and how he sold them; how the Apostles ate, travelled, slept, worked, talked, conversed, and so forth. The great actions of those who are not saints are very small and low in the eyes of God, Who regards as great those which the Saints perform in His honour ; Who regards them as great, however humble they be.

> Works done with Charity are never ill :
> Works done without her nought can skill.

"*The Spirit of the Blessed Francis de Sales, Bishop of Geneva,*" *by the Bishop of Belley. Burns & Oates.*

IT was not only to mankind that Francis showed himself so sweet and good—his kindness extended even to animals. He never hurt them, and, as much as was in his power, prevented others from doing so, saying that pity for animals was part of natural goodness, and that those who were gentle with them would be still more so towards mankind ; and, on the contrary, those who did any of them harm for pleasure only, and wantonly, gave proof of a bad heart.

"*Vie de François de Sales, Evêque et Prince de Genève.*" *Par le Curé de St. Sulpice. Vol. II. Paris : Jacques Lecoffre et Cie,* 1856.

SAINT JOSEPH OF CUPERTINO.

It was a most wonderful thing to see with what readiness irrational creatures obeyed him. A linnet, to which he said often : "Praise God!" praised Him with its song at a signal from the Saint, and ceased immediately when told to do so. In setting a goldfinch free : "Go," he said to it, "enjoy that which God has given you. I desire nothing more of you than that you should return when I call you, that we may praise together your God and mine."

Obedient to his word, the little bird flew into the neighbouring orchard, and when recalled by St. Joseph, he at once returned to sing with him the greatness of the Creator.

A kite, which had killed a goldfinch of which he was very fond, because it repeated what he had taught it : "Jesu Maria. Brother Joseph, say the office," turned at once at his voice, saw him, and hearing itself reproved by him thus : "Oh, scoundrel, you have killed my goldfinch, and you deserve that I should kill you!" it seemed sorry for its crime, and went on to the top of the cage, and remained there, till St. Joseph, slapping it with his hand, said: "Go; I pardon you."

A ram, bitten by mad dogs, became mad, and was shut up in a little orchard that it might not hurt anyone. The servant of the Lord by chance entered into the enclosure, and when cautioned to be on his guard against the creature, he smiled, and said he had confidence in God. Then he turned to the ram, and touching it, said: "Mad as thou art, what art thou doing here? Return to the flock." He then let it go free, and it at once became sane and submissive to the shepherd.

Equally marvellous was the obedience of a little white lamb sent by St. Joseph to the nuns of St. Clare of Cupertino. It almost seemed to follow exactly the observances of the monastery. It was always the first at all the functions, very sparing in its eating, quiet in the choir, and solely anxious to arouse with blows and shakings those who were drowsy, or to tear off with its feet and teeth any vain apparel which it saw. After the death of the lamb, the Saint said he would send the same holy virgins a little bird, that it might serve as an incitement to them to praise God; and thus it came to pass, during the time of divine service, a solitary sparrow flew in through the window of the choir, and began to sing gently there.

The miracle did not end there, because, one day, seeing two novices in dispute, the bird came between them, doing all it could with outstretched wings and with its little claws to keep them apart and to calm them. But being ill-used by one of them, and driven away, it went off, and, notwithstanding its fixed habits of five years' standing, it did not return. The sisters, being very sorry for this, asked St. Joseph about it. He said: "It is well; you have hurt it and driven it away? It will not return to you." Then, touched by their prayers, he promised to send it back;

and at the first sound of the choir the bird returned not only to sing at the window, but to become still more at home in the monastery. Their astonishment increased still more when the nuns, having for their amusement tied a little bell to its leg, it did not appear on Holy Thursday and Good Friday. So they again had recourse to St. Joseph, who said: "I send it to you to sing, and not to ring a bell. It has not come, because it has been these two days watching the Sepulchre. But I will send it back to you." And, in fact, the little creature returned, and remained with them a long time.

Two hares in the vicinity of the Convent of the Grotto obeyed the voice of the Saint, who said to them: "Do not leave the vicinity of the Church of the Madonna, because there are many hunters who come very near it."

They did well to obey him, because one of them, pursued by the huntsmen, fled into the church, and thence into the convent, and when it found St. Joseph, it jumped into his arms, and he said to it: "Did I not tell you that you should not go far from the church, or you would lose your skin?" And he saved it from its pursuers, who laid claim to it. Its companion was equally fortunate, for being pursued by hounds it took refuge under Brother Joseph's tunic. Soon after, the Marquis of Cupertino, who was the principal huntsman, happened to ask Brother Joseph if he had seen the hare: "Here it is," he replied. "Do not give yourself more trouble about it." Then "Go," he said to the animal, "save yourself in these bushes; and you, do not move." The hare obeyed him. The hounds remained stationary, and the Marquis and his companions remained overwhelmed with astonishment at the miracle.

"*Compendio della Vita, Virtù e Miracoli del B. Giuseppe di Copertino, Sac. Profess. dell' Ordine de' Minori Conventuali di S. Francesco.*" Dedicated to *His Holiness Pope Benedict XIV. Rome, MDCCLIII.*

SAINT BASSIAN,

Bishop of Lodi, A.D. 413.

QUITTING Syracuse and Sicily at an early age, in order to go and be baptised at Ravenna, he met a doe with her two fawns, pursued by huntsmen. The mother, mad with fear, cowered with her fawns close to St. Bassian. One of the huntsmen wished to kill the animals in spite of the traveller who protected them; but he became suddenly possessed by the devil. Is this not a type of the protection which, when he became Bishop, the Saint was to show afterwards to the weak?

The town of Corvio alleges that this event took place not far from its walls, and it is to perpetuate the memory of the event that it has put a deer in its coat of arms.

"*The Little Bollandists.*"

ST. HUBERT'S VISION OF THE CRUCIFIX IN THE HORNS OF THE HUNTED STAG.
(*Albert Dürer.*) See p. 63.

SAINT HUBERT.

SAINT HUBERT, when hunting in the Forest of Ardennes, encountered a milk-white stag, and beheld a crucifix in its horns. Falling on his knees, he forbore to continue his sport, and renouncing all others, he became a Hermit in this same forest. And yet he is called the Patron of Hunters until this day!

SAINT THEONAS,

Man of Letters and Anchorite (fourth century).

THE sick crowded to the cell of the *Prophet*, as he was called. He used to appear at the window of his cell, extending his hand, and blessing and healing the crowd, and withdraw without a word. At night he crossed the threshold of his impenetrable dwelling. This was to give the beasts of God, the animals of the desert, the clear water of his fountain. This was why his cell was always surrounded by stout buffaloes, light-footed goats, and bounding wild asses, which seemed to form a guard of honour round the friend of God and also of nature.

SAINT ALDEBRAND,

Bishop and Patron of Fossombrone (Twelfth century.)

He had abstained from meat all his life, and when in his old age they thought of serving him up a roast partridge to strengthen his stomach, he blessed the bird, and ordered it to fly away through the air, which it at once hastened to do.

SAINT FRAIMBAUD OF AUVERGNE,

Recluse, Patron of Ivry in the Diocese of Paris.

The reputation of Fraimbaud increased from day to day, and the more he fled from honour, the more honour pursued him. His new miracles contributed greatly to bring him into general admiration, for he cured the sick, he restored sight to the blind, raised the dead, cast out evil spirits from the bodies of the possessed, calmed storms, caused the plague and other contagious diseases to cease, and obtained children, riches, and other benefits for those who implored his help with humility and faith. One might have said that God had determined to refuse none of his prayers. Every day the birds of the forest near his monastery came to rejoice his spirit with their songs, until he blessed and sent them away. One day he noticed that they were sad when he dismissed them. He followed them to see what caused their sorrow, and he found them surrounding the little body of one of their companions. Moved with pity, Fraimbaud extended his hand, made the sign of the Cross, and the bird was restored to life.

SAINT CASTOR OF NISMES.

Founder and Abbot of Mananque.

IN pictures of St. Castor of Nismes, we generally see a wild boar near him. This is to commemorate the fact that one day, when he was entering the episcopal city, one of these animals, pursued by hounds, came close to the man of God, who secured the safety of its life.

SAINT GALL OF IRELAND.

Founder and First Abbot of the Monastery of the Benedictines of St. Gall, in Switzerland.

AFTER his restoration to health, love of solitude induced him to seek some other retreat than that of Bregenz, and he applied to Hiltibal, deacon of Willimar, for advice, as he had an intimate knowledge of all the country round. When they had prayed, the two pilgrims took their meal with thanksgiving at sunset, then having prayed again, they lay down on the ground to rest a little. When the holy man thought his companion was asleep, he prostrated himself before the reliquary with arms outstretched, and prayed to God with great devotion. However, a bear, coming down from the mountain, carefully gathered up the crumbs left by the two companions. The man of God seeing what the beast was doing, said to it: "I order you, in the name of Our Lord Jesus Christ, to take some wood, and put it on the fire." At this command, the animal went to take a large piece of wood, and put it on the fire. Whereupon the Saint took a loaf of bread out of the satchel, and gave it to this new servant, saying: "In the name of Our Lord Jesus Christ, leave this valley, and share with us the surrounding mountains and hills, on condition that you do no harm to man or beast." The deacon, who pretended to be asleep, was contemplating with astonishment all that was taking place. . . .

SAINT COLETTE,

Reformer of the Three Orders of St. Francis.

FROM the *Life of St. Colette*, edited, in the year 1448, by her last confessor, Pierre de Vaux, one of the reformed friars:

Once a beautiful little lark was brought to her—called a lark (*alouette*), some say, because of the praises it sings to God, and also because it lives without stores, according to the poverty of the saints. She took such a great pleasure in it, and saw it so gladly, that when she took a meal, the little lark took it with her, and ate and drank it with her, as if she were a bird like itself. Very often many pure and beautiful birds came near her oratory, and approached so close to her that she could take hold of them as they sang their sweet songs. They took their little meals more familiarly and peacefully with her than they would have done among birds of their own kind in the forest, and that because she resembled them in purity.

Once a lovely little lamb was brought to her as an offering of piety, and she accepted it alike for its purity, and because it was an emblem of the Lamb without stain or sin. Many a time her spirit was consoled and comforted by it, so much the more, because every time it was present at the elevation of the Host, it, without being told, went on its knees, and thus adored its Blessed Creator.

SAINT JOSSE.

His life was so pure that it seemed as if the privileges of the terrestrial Paradise were revived for him. Animals did not flee from him; but, on the contrary, birds and fishes would come and eat out of his hand in a familiar way.

SAINT RIQUIER, ABBOT.

Even the animals (says Hariulfe) showed an affectionate trust in him. When the Saint was eating, the birds surrounded him, perched upon his knees and shoulders, and, when they had received some crumbs of bread, they showed their joyous gratitude by their songs, and by flapping their wings.

"*Hagiographie du Diocèse d'Amiens.*" *Par L'Abbé Corblet. Tome i., Paris, J. B. Dumolin.*

SAINT QUÉ.

SAINT QUÉ was an Irish hermit who came to Brittany. It is said that he was consecrated Bishop, October 7th, 495. Near him we find a cart drawn by eight deer. A hunted deer had thrown itself into the Saint's hermitage, and he refused to give up the refugee. The huntsman (a Celtic noble), in his anger, claimed compensation for losing it by laying his hands on some oxen and a cow, which were all the cattle belonging to the monastery. Next day, eight stags came and offered themselves to the servant of God, in order to replace the domestic animals which saving the life of one of their kind had cost him.

BISHOP ALBERT OF SIENA,

ONE day he was working in the country, and a hare which was near him allowed itself to be taken; and, later on, the same animal, chased by hunters, fled towards the man of God, who slipped it into his sleeve until its pursuers were gone. Then he let it go free to return to its lair. It is said that, when his brethren seemed to wish to make use of this game, he replied, "We took no trouble to take it, and it has done us no harm; by what right should we appropriate it?"

SAINT GERARD DE BROGNE.

THE Saint, who was travelling, continued his fast while his companions took their meal, giving as his excuse that he must have fish, when a fish was flung at his feet by a bird of prey. This unexpected provision removed his excuse for mortification, which Providence, doubtless, judged to be unwise. But the man of God wanted to reserve at least a part of the fish, so that the bird of prey might be able to carry something to its young ones.

"*Emblems of the Saints in Popular Art.*" Enumerated and explained by Father Ch. Cahier, of the Society of Jesus. Vols. I. and II. Paris: Poussielgue Frères, 1867.

SAINT SOLANGE.

HER sheep had no need of blows to guide them. If they sometimes wandered into the fields around, the young shepherdess had no occasion to run after them, nor to frighten them with her cries nor to chase them with her crook; but, quite quietly and gently, without angry cries, she called them, as the angels might, by the simple, inward exercise of her will; she had only to seek for them with the eyes of her soul, and they quickly ran to her and encircled their sweet mistress.

The birds of the fields flew round her without fear, and as, later on, the "birds of the hoary woods" settled on the shoulders of the shepherdess of Domremy, so they rested on the shoulders and fair hair of the virgin of Villemond, and we may believe that they conversed as brothers with the angelic sister.

"*Histoire de Ste. Solange, Vierge et Martyre, Patronne de Berry.*" Par *l'Abbè Joseph Bernard. Société Générale de Libraires Catholiques, Paris,* 1879.

SAINT BERNARD.

When God created man's heart, says Bossuet, the first thing he put in it was goodness. Like all noble natures, Bernard made the best use of this splendid gift: kindness with him dominated all other feelings. This man, so hard to himself, could not contemplate pain or weakness without feeling immense compassion. Nothing that was human was strange to him. To the living he gave advice, consolation, care, and remedies; to the dead he gave prayers and tears—it was remarked that he never could attend the funeral of a stranger without weeping. His biographer tells us that his humanity extended to irrational animals and to wild beasts. At the sight of a hare pursued by hounds, or of a little bird threatened by a bird of prey, his heart was rent: he could not help making the sign of the Cross in the air, in order to save the innocent little things; and his blessing always brought them happiness.

We may remember the beautiful words he used in one of his letters: "If pity were a sin, I could not help committing it."

"*Life of St. Bernard, Abbot of Clairvaux.*" By the Abbot E. Vacandard, Doctor in Theology. Vol. II. Paris: Victor Lecoffre, 1895.

He was so humane that he sympathised not only with his fellow creatures, but also with irrational animals, birds, and wild beasts; and his sympathy was shown in its excellent results. For it sometimes happened that on a journey, by making the sign of the cross he miraculously released a hare, pursued by dogs and apparently on the point of being caught (or a bird chased by hawks). And he used to tell the hunters that their efforts would be in vain, for they would secure no prey while he was present.

Acta Sanct. Ed. noviss. Aug. Tom. IV.

BLESSED GERARD MAJELLA.

BLESSED GERARD had only to call the little birds, and they came and perched on his hands. A nephew of the Arch-priest, Don Salvador of Oliveto, had a little bird in a cage. Gerard, after having caressed it, set it free. At the sight of the bird flying away, the child uttered piercing cries. In order to quiet him, the good brother went to the window. "Return," said he; "return little bird, because the child is crying." At once the bird came and perched on the hand of the servant of God, who restored it to the child.

One day, when he was at table in our Convent of Caposito, he made a sign with his hand, and thus called the birds which were chirping in the vicinity. The charming little creatures, obedient to the orders of him who served his God so faithfully, came at once and flew round the Saint, and placed themselves on the table in front of him. They fixed their eyes on his, and seemed to lend an attentive ear to the words of kindness, gentleness, and simplicity which he addressed to them, as if they understood him perfectly.

"*Le Thaumaturge du XVIII. Siècle : ou La Vie du Bienheureux Gérard Majella.*" Par Père S. Omer, Redemptoriste, Liége. Desclée, de Brower et Cie, 1893.

SAINT KEVIN,

Abbot of Glendalough and Patron of Dublin.

SAINT COERNGHAN (or Kevin), Abbot, Patron of Dublin, was born about the year 500, of a princely family, whose territory lay near the sea-shore, in the present county of Wicklow. For him, as for other saints, part of the lost empire of Paradise was restored, as the wild beasts of the mountains and the forest became tame in his presence, and drank out of his hand. Among many other examples, we are told, for instance, that on one occasion a wild boar, tracked by the hounds of King Brandub's huntsmen, burst into his little oratory. The Saint was praying under a tree, with birds of different kinds perched on his hand and shoulders, or flying round him, singing their gayest notes, for even the boughs and leaves were musical for the Saint of God. The hounds crouched before the oratory, but dared not enter, and the huntsman, Enna, the ancester of the Kinsellas, awed by the miracle, drew them away. For this, or a similar reason, St. Kevin has always been represented in pictures, in the ancient churches, with a bird on his hand. In the *Leabhar na Geeart*, St. Kevin appears entitled to nearly the same honours as St. Brigid from the Kings of ancient Leinster, a territory co-extensive with the present ecclesiastical province of Dublin.

"*Calendar of the Irish Saints.*" *By the Rev. Matthew Kelly, D.D., Professor of Ecclesiastical History, St. Patrick's College, Maynooth. Dublin: J. Mullany.*

THE holy Kevin, while avoiding the society of his fellow men during the season of Lent, as his custom was, devoted his time to reading and prayers, in the desert, occupying a small hut which did nothing but keep out the sun and rain, giving himself up to contemplation only. And while he was lifting up his hand to heaven through the window, as he used to do, a blackbird by chance alighted on it, and treating it as a nest, laid an egg there. And the Saint showed such compassion towards it, out of his patient and loving heart, that he neither closed his hand nor withdrew it, but indefatigably held it out and adapted it for the purpose until the young one was fully hatched. And, in order to perpetuate the memory of this wonderful act, all the figures of St. Kevin, throughout Ireland, have a blackbird sitting on his open hand.

SAINT GERTRUDE.

She was touched by such a feeling of tender affection, not only for mankind, but also for the whole of the animal creation, that if she saw any creature, whether bird or beast, suffering from hunger, thirst, or cold, she was soon deeply affected to the core of her heart by a fellow-feeling for her Lord's living handiwork, and reverently offered, as well as she could, the poor irrational creature's suffering to the Lord, to His eternal praise, in union with that dignity wherewith He has so highly perfected and ennobled all His creatures, begging the Lord to have mercy on His creature, and to be pleased to remedy its ills.

"*Revelationes Gertrudianæ ac Mechtildianæ*," vol. i., p. 26. *Apud Henricum Oudin.* 1875.

BISHOP NEMEDIUS.

It is the duty of a ruler to employ his subjects according to the measure of his necessities, and not to misuse them with intemperance and insolence for his own selfish pleasure, nor to be burdensome and oppressive to them. Therefore, those who do not treat animals properly are greatly at fault; for they do not fulfil the duties of a ruler, or even those of a just man, since, as it is recorded in Holy Scripture, "The upright has compassion on the souls of his beasts of burden."

Patrologiæ Græcæ (Migne). Tom. XL. Patres Ægypti: Nemesii Episcopi Emesæ, "De Natura Hominis."

SAINT BLASIUS.

The faithful who lived in Sebaste, a city of Cappadocia, witnessing his irreproachable life, chose him as their Bishop. But he went to a mountain called Argeum, and lived in a cave, and wild beasts came to him; and, if any of them happened to be in pain, they flocked to the Saint in his cave, as if they were rational creatures, and would not leave him until he had laid his hands on them and blessed them.

In those days, Agricolaus, the Governor, ordered the wild beasts to be gathered together, and the hunters also came to the mountain in which St. Blasius the Bishop lived. On seeing the cave, and the crowd of beasts standing before it, they looked at one another in alarm and astonishment, and exclaimed, "What is the meaning of this?" And, on approaching the cave, they found St. Blasius praying. So they returned, and told the Governor what they had seen; but the Governor, on hearing of it, ordered more soldiers to go with them to bring before him as many Christians as they found there in hiding.

Acta Sanct.; Ed. Noviss. Feb. Tom. I.

SAINT MACARIUS.

THE servant of God, Paphnutius, the disciple of this renowned Saint, tells us that, while Macarius was one day sitting in his cell and addressing God, a hyæna caught up her cub, which was blind, and brought it to him. She knocked at the door of his cell with her head, and entered while he was sitting there, and laid her cub at his feet. Whereupon St. Macarius took up the cub, spat on its eyes, and prayed to God ; and immediately its sight was restored. Its mother then suckled it, and carried it off. On the following day she brought Macarius the skin of a large sheep ; but, when the Saint saw the skin, he addressed the hyæna as follows : " How did you obtain this, if not by devouring somebody's sheep? and I refuse to accept the proceeds of wrong-doing as a present from you." But the hyæna bent her head to the ground, and, kneeling before the feet of the Saint, laid the skin before him. But he said to her : " I tell you I will not accept it, unless you swear you will never again injure the poor by eating their sheep." The hyæna at this again inclined her head, as if in assent to the command of St. Macarius. Then he took the skin from the hyæna. But the blessed servant of God, Melania, told me she received that skin from Macarius, which used to be called "The Hyæna's Gift."

What wonder is it if, among men crucified to the world, a hyæna, from a deep sense of gratitude, brought gifts to the glory of God and the honour of His Saints? For the same God who, in the Book of Daniel the Prophet, tamed lions, bestowed understanding also on this hyæna.

Acta Sanct.; Ed. Noviss. Jan. Tom. I.

SAINT SULPICIUS SEVERUS.

WE see another equally remarkable man, who used to dwell in a small cell, which was only large enough for one. It was reported that a wolf used to come to him at supper, and hardly ever failed to make its appearance before him at the usual hour of his repast, waiting before the door till he presented it with the bread left over from his meal. It used to lick his hand, and then leave him, as if by so doing it had fulfilled its duty, and comforted him. By chance, it happened that while the Saint was seeing off a Brother who had come to him, he was absent a long time, and did not return till dark.

Meanwhile, the beast made its way to the cell at the usual hour of supper. But when it found its kind friend was not there, it entered the empty cell and searched diligently for its occupier. A basket was hanging there containing five loaves of bread, so it took one of them and ate it up; and then, its misdeed accomplished, it went away. The hermit, however, on his return, saw the basket open, and that the number of loaves was incomplete. He perceived his loss of private belongings, and noticed then the crumbs of the stolen loaf near the door: but he had no doubt as to who had made off with it. When the beast did not appear on the following day, as was its custom (wonderful to relate, its conscience smote it for its bold action, and it gave up coming to him to whom it had done the wrong), the hermit was much distressed, because he was deprived of the companionship of his visitor. However, he recalled it by his prayers, and it arrived on the seventh day, as it was wont to do previously, at supper-time. But you may easily recognise the shame of the penitent, for it did not dare to approach as near as before, but cast its eyes down to the ground in abject confusion (which could be easily seen), as if it was imploring pardon. And so the hermit, out of pity for its distress of mind, bade it come nearer, and gently stroked the poor beast's head, and repaired its fault by replacing the loaf. And so it obtained pardon, laid aside its grief, and resumed its customary office of ministering to the hermit.

Behold, I pray you, the power of Christ in this incident, who imparts intelligence to brutes and gentleness to wild animals! The she-wolf renders kindly services, acknowledges the charge of theft, and is humbled with shame at the thought of what it has done; and, on being summoned, it approaches, and proffers its head, and has a sense of pardon received, as if it was ashamed of its misdeeds. This is Thy power, O Christ, and these are Thy wonderful works! for what Thy servants do in Thy name is Thine. But we grieve over the fact that Thy Majesty is felt by beasts, but is not revered by men.

Now, lest perchance this may appear to anyone hard to believe, I will tell you of greater things. Upon my word, as a true Christian, I am not inventing nor repeating stories of doubtful authenticity; but I will set down what I have ascertained from men of trust. There are men called anchorites, living mostly in the deserts, without any dwellings; they feed on roots, and never stay in the same place, for fear they should be visited by men. Wherever night overtakes them, there they rest. Now, two Monks from Nitria, a very distant region, came to a certain man who lived under this *régime*, because in days gone by he had been an intimate friend when living in a monastery, and they had heard of his holy life. For a long time they sought him, but at last they found him, in the seventh month, living in a remote part of the desert near Blembi, which lonely district he was reported to have inhabited for twelve years. Now, although he avoided intercourse with all men, he did not, however, deny himself to those with whom he was acquainted, but for three days associated with his friends. On the fourth day he went a little distance while accompanying his friends on their homeward journey, and they saw a huge lioness approach him. Now, although the beast had met with three men, she was in no doubt as to whom she was seeking, but cast herself at the feet of the anchorite, and, by a kind of whining and wailing, began to show signs, not only of grief, but of a petition to urge. All were touched at the sight, and especially the one who knew he was wanted. They then followed the lioness, who went before them, and, as she led the way, halting every now and then and looking back, they could easily see that she wanted the anchorite to follow wherever she led him. Why should I make a long story of it? They arrived at the beast's cave, where she was suckling five full-grown cubs with difficulty, because she was expecting another litter.

These cubs had been blind from their birth, and the beast brought them down, one by one, from the rock, and laid them at the feet of the Anchorite. Thereupon the Saint understood what the beast was asking for ; and so he called on the name of God, and placed his hands on the cubs' closed eyes, and they were opened upon the light which had been so long denied. And so those Brothers, after their visit to the beloved anchorite, returned home with a very instructive reward for their labours, from the fact of having witnessed the faith of the Saint and the glory of Christ, to which they were to bear witness in proof of his greatly reputed holiness.

Patrol. Curs. Com. Tom. XX. Parisiis: 1845.
Sulpicii Severi Dialogi, Dial. i.

SAINT ADAMNAN,

Abbot of Iona.

A Brother, by name Molua, grandson of Brennus, came to the Saint while he was writing and said to him: "Please bless this weapon in my hand." So he raised his holy hand a little and blessed it, making the sign of the cross with his pen, his face meanwhile being turned towards the book upon which he was writing. As the aforesaid Brother was on the point of departing with the weapon which had been blessed, the Saint enquired: "What kind of a weapon have I blessed for the Brother?" Diarmid, his faithful servant, replied: "A dagger for cutting the throats of oxen and bulls." But the former said in response: "I trust in my God that the weapon which I blessed will injure neither man nor beast." And the Saint's words proved true that very hour. For after the same Brother had left the monastery enclosure and wanted to kill an ox, he made the attempt with three strong blows and a vigorous thrust, but could not pierce its skin. And when the monks became acquainted with it, they melted the metal of the same dagger by the heat of the fire, and anointed with it all the iron weapons of the monastery; and they were thereafter unable to inflict a wound on any flesh in consequence of the abiding power of the Saint's blessing.

Acta Sanct.; Ed. Noviss. Junii. Tom. II.

SAINT GUTHLAC OF CROYLAND.

In the aforementioned island two portentous ravens used to live, and their mischievousness was so vexatious that whatever they could break or destroy or tear asunder, or plunder, or pollute, they ruined with utter recklessness. For they would enter a house, with their well-known cries, and plunder whatever they found within or without. But the above-mentioned Servant of God put up with their various misdeeds, and endured them with long suffering in his holy heart, so that he not only afforded an example of patience amongst men, but displayed it to birds and beasts. For the grace of his rare charity abounded towards all things, so that the birds of that uncultivated wilderness and the migratory fishes of the miry lake swam or flew quickly to him at his call, and came to him as to a shepherd. From his hand they were fed as the nature of each required.

Acta Sanct.; Ed. Noviss. Aprilis. Tom. II.

SAINT ANSELM,

Archbishop of Canterbury and Doctor of the Church.

As Anselm was leaving the Palace and was going to his country residence, called Heyses, the boys whom he was bringing up set the dogs after a hare which had crossed their path. And they followed it up till, in its flight, it sank exhausted beneath the feet of the horse which the Father himself was riding. And because he knew that the poor creature had thus fled to him for refuge, he pulled in the reins and stopped his horse, and would not refuse the beast the protection it sought. The dogs surrounded it, and with unwelcome attention licked it all over, but they could neither drive it from under the horse nor do it any harm. We looked on in astonishment; but when Anselm saw some of the huntsmen begin to laugh and indulge in excessive joy because they regarded the beast as captured, he burst into tears and said: "Do you laugh? It is no laughing matter for this poor creature." At these words he rode on and continued his journey, forbidding his dogs, in a loud voice, to follow the hare any more. Thereupon, seeing it was free from all ill-treatment, it ran quickly to its old haunts, amidst fields and woods. We, however, ceased to joke, and, quite happy at such a kindly release of a frightened animal, went our way.

Another time he saw a boy playing with a young bird on the road. But it had its legs tied with a piece of string, and when the boy slackened it, it tried to fly away, wishing to escape. But the boy held the string in his hands and dragged it back to his feet, and this afforded him great sport. He did it over and over again. But when the Father saw it he was grieved, and felt deeply for the bird, and wished the string to break and the bird to be free again. And, behold, the string breaks, and the bird flies away: the boy weeps, but the Father rejoices.

Acta Sanct.; Ed. Noviss. Aprilis. Tom. II.;

SAINT BARTHOLOMEW OF FARNE ISLAND.

FROM of yore it is told that certain birds live in this island, and that it miraculously preserves both their name and race. At nesting time they assemble there, and they soon acquire such wonderful tameness from the sanctity of the place, or rather from those who have sanctified the place by their holy life, that they are not afraid of being touched or gazed at by human beings. They love quiet, but are not alarmed by noise. Once upon a time a bird was leading out her young, when one of them fell into the depths of a cleft rock. Its mother stood still in her grief, clearly showing signs of human intelligence. For she at once left her young on the spot, and returned to Bartholomew, and began to drag him by the hem of his coat with her beak, as if plainly to say: "Rise, and follow me, and give me back my offspring." Thereupon he quickly arose, thinking she was trying to find her nest beneath him. But she dragged at his robe more and more, and at last he perceived that she wanted something which she could not express in words. Although she was unable to speak, she knew well how to act. He then followed, the bird leading; and when she reached the rock she showed him the place with her beak, and looked up to Bartholomew, asking him as plainly as she could to look into the chasm. When he approached he saw the little bird clinging to the rock with its wings, so he descended the chasm and restored it to its mother. And she was so delighted as to appear to show her thanks by the cheerfulness of her expression. She then entered the water with her young, and Bartholomew, filled with amazement, returned to his oratory. Thus at all times the Lord of all excellence distributes His grace unto His Saints, so that often the most trivial things increase their claim to still greater grace.

Acta Sanct.; Ed. Noviss. Junii. Tom. V.

SAINT THOMAS AQUINAS,

Now as regards the exercise of the feelings, the heart of man is moved even towards animals; for because the sense of pity is aroused by the sufferings of others, and it happens that brute beasts feel pain, the feeling of pity can be aroused in man even for the sufferings of animals. But the next thing to remark about it is that he who shews pity to animals is more disposed to exercise the same feeling towards his fellow creatures. Hence it is said, Proverbs

12, 10: "The upright knows the souls of his own beasts, but the heart of the wicked is cruel." And so, in order that the Lord might incline the hearts of the Jews to pity, a nation which was prone to cruelty, he wished them to get into the habit of showing compassion even to brute beasts, by forbidding certain things which seemed to come under the head of cruelty. Hence he forbade a kid to be cooked in its mother's milk, or an ox to be muzzled while treading out the corn, or the mother to be killed with her young.

St. Thomas Aqu., O.P., Doct. Angel. et Omnium Scholarum Catholicarum Patroni Summa Theol. Ed. Eminentiss. Card. Josephi Pecci Oblata. Tom. II. Paris, 1887.

THE GENTLENESS OF SAINTS.

SAINT CHRYSOSTOM, in his Epistle to the Romans, chap. xxix., speaks as follows: "The souls of the Saints are excessively gentle and loving to men—not only to their own people, but to strangers, and they show this gentleness even to brute beasts." Therefore, also a certain wise man has said: "The just man is merciful to the lives of his beasts of burden."

If, therefore, of beasts of burden, much more of men. The same Chrysostom explains this passage at greater length in his *Catena Græca*: "What do I hear?" says he. "Does the just man pity the souls of his beasts of burden?" Then surely we ought to show to them great gentleness and kindness for many reasons, but for this above all: that we may take by this means an opportunity to sympathise with them, because they are of the same origin as ourselves. For not without reason in the Law does God bid us raise up the beast of burden which has fallen, and bring back into the path the straying sheep, and not muzzle the ox which treads out the corn. He wishes us, therefore, to show great mercy to brute beasts.

God, therefore, commanded the Jews to be merciful to beasts of burden, that they might learn to be merciful to their neighbours, for fear that, if they were cruel to their beasts, they would learn to be cruel to their fellow-men. But God gave his sanction to this pity, not only by word, but also by example. For He Himself has a care for beasts, whence that passage in the Psalms, xxxv. 7: "Thou Lord shalt save both man and beast." And Christ, says St. Bernard, was placed in the manger between an ox and an ass, that he might save man and beast. And Psalm ciii. 14: "Bringing forth food for the cattle" And Psalm cxlvi. 9: "Who giveth food to cattle and feedeth the young ravens that call upon Him." Those, therefore, who are compassionate towards animals imitate God and his loving kindness. So St. Anselm, as is recorded in his Life, was moved with feeling of pity towards brute beasts, and used to weep for them when he saw them caught in the hunters' nets. St. Francis says wonderful things about a cricket, a pheasant, a falcon, and wolves, beloved and protected by this saintly man, and summoned by him to glorify God.

Cornelius a Lapide. Burns & Oates.

THE TERM "CREATURE."

"For the earnest expectation of the creature waiteth for the manifestation of the sons of God."—*Rom.* viii. 19.

THE term "creature" is here most happily employed. For in verse 22 it is opposed to men and the sons of God. And so it is used by SS. Chrysostom, Theodoret, Theophylact, Œcumenius, Ambrose (Book iv., Hexameron), Hilary (Book xii. on the Trinity), Sotus, Adamus, Pererius, and Toletus.

"*The creature was made subject to vanity, not willingly but by reason of him who hath subjected the same in hope*" (*Ib.* v. 20). "In hope," that is, of being freed, and of a change for the better in the general resurrection and renewal of men and all things.

"*The creature shall be freed from the slavery of corruption into the glorious liberty of the children of God*" (*Ib.* v. 21). "Into the liberty," *i.e.*, evidently into the imitation, or after the pattern, of the liberty of the sons of God, that other creatures may receive a similar liberty enduring and immortal. "Into," therefore, denotes a pattern or even cause. So say Pererius and Toletus.

Note: The liberty of glory is the same as

glorious liberty. Secondly, the liberty is not of nature nor of grace, but of glory, and is a state of freedom from all wretchedness and weakness and suffering and corruption, as well as from all evil of mind and body, and guilt and penalty.

Cornelius a Lapide. Burns & Oates.

SAINT MARBON OF TOURS.

As he was once making the round of his province, he came upon a party of huntsmen. The dogs were following a hare, and the poor beast was worn out with a long run, and, being unable to make its escape owing to the wide extent of the open fields, and on the point of being caught, made many a double in order to escape immediate death. Now this blessed man, with a deep sense of pity for its danger, ordered the dogs to stop following it and to allow it to escape. They forthwith stopped at the very first word of his command. One would have thought they came to a standstill because they had been tied, or rather rooted, to the spot.

Patrol. Census Compl. J. P. Migne. Series Prima. Patrol XX. Parisiis, 1845. Sulpicii Severi Dialogi. D. II.

SAINT LAUMER.

The holy man carried out these works of dutiful affection, not only towards men but even to wild and brute beasts.

Acta Sanct.; Ed. Noviss. Jan. Tom. II.

SAINT GREGORY THE GREAT ON SS. EUTYCHIUS AND FLORENTIUS.

At the same time two men, the former of whom was named Eutychius and the latter Florentius, lived the life of a holy calling, in a district of the province of Nursia. Now the same Eutychius devoted himself to the practice of his religion with fervent zeal, and by the earnestness of his exhortation won the souls of many to God. Florentius, on the other hand, passed his days in simple living and prayer. Now, there was a monastery not far off, which was bereft owing to the death of the Abbot; wherefore the monks wanted the same Eutychius to preside over them. So he complied with their entreaties and ruled over the monastery for many years, and exercised the souls of his disciples in the practice of holy living. But in order that the oratory, where he formerly lived, should not be deserted, he left the venerable Florentius there. And as he lived there by himself, one day he was occupied in prayer, and entreated Almighty God to be pleased to send him some solace in his dwelling. When he had finished his prayer, and had left the oratory, he found a bear before his door. And, by its bending down its head to the ground and exhibiting nothing savage in its demeanour, it plainly showed that it came to attend on the man of God, which he at once recognised. Now, in the same cell were four or five out of a flock which had no one to feed or look after them, so he commanded the bear and said: "Go and lead out these sheep and return at 12 o'clock," which the bear immediately proceeded to do. The bear was, therefore, entrusted with the office of shepherd, and the same hungry beast which used to devour sheep began now to feed them. When the man of God wished to fast until about three o'clock, he ordered the bear to return at the same hour; but when he did not wish to fast so late it was to come back at mid-day. The bear obeyed the man of God in all things, so that when told to return at noon it did not come at three o'clock, nor when told to return at three did it come at noon. Seeing that this occurred for a long time, the reputation of his great holiness began to spread far and wide in that same locality.

But just as the old enemy, from whatever quarter he sees the good proceeding to greater glory, from the same quarter plunges the wicked through envy into torment, so four men of the disciples of the venerable Eutychius, out of bitter envy because their master did not work miracles, and because he who had been left alone by Eutychius seemed to be raised far above him by so great a miracle, lay in wait for the same bear and killed it. And when it did not appear at the bidden time, the man of God, Florentius, became doubtful of its return. He waited for it till evening, and began to be distressed because the bear, which, in his thoroughly unaffected way, he used to call his brother, did not return. The next day, however, he went into the fields to look for both bear and sheep, the former of which he found slain; but, upon making careful enquiry, he soon discovered by whom it had been killed. Then he abandoned himself to grief in lamenting over the malice of the Brothers, rather than the death of the bear.

Now, the venerable Eutychius had been summoned to console him, but the same man of God, in his presence, under the influence of his great grief, cursed these Brothers, saying : " I hope to God Almighty that they who put to death my bear, which did no harm to them, will, in this life, have vengeance repaid to them before the eyes of all." And Divine retribution followed these words forthwith. For the four monks who had killed the same bear were immediately stricken with such a severe attack of leprosy that their limbs rotted away and they died, at which the man of God, Florentius, was greatly alarmed, and was afraid because he had so cursed the

Brothers. He never ceased to weep for the rest of his life because his prayer had been granted, and he exclaimed that he was vindictive and guilty of their death.

Acta Sanct.; Ed. Noviss. Majii. Tom. V.

SAINT ELIAS.

THE SAINT had a deep feeling of pity and kindness, not only towards those gifted with reason and of the same nature as himself, but also to animals destitute of a reasonable soul and intellect.

Acta Sanct.; Ed. Noviss. Sept. Tom. III.

ST. GILES RECEIVING THROUGH HIS HAND THE ARROW AIMED AT THE HIND.
(*Flemish School.*) See p. viii.

SAINT PATRICK,

Apostle and Patron of Ireland.

A NOBLE man, named Darius, wishing to show greater favour to the holy Bishop, Saint Patrick, brought him from a humbler place to a higher one, and from a narrow spot to a grand and pleasant one called Druymsaileach, which was afterwards named Armagh, and which was pointed out to him beforehand by a heavenly miracle. While St. Patrick was going round it and pondering over the pleasantness and suitableness of the spot he found a stag with its hind lying there, and his companions wanted to kill it, but the holy Father forbade them to do so. And in order to show the strong affection which he felt towards God's creatures, the holy Father took up the aforesaid hind in his arms and stroked it with his hands, and caressed it, and carried it to a glade situated towards the north part of Armagh. The stag, too, as meekly as any sheep, followed the kind-hearted bearer of the burden until its hind was put down and set free.

Acta Sanct.; Ed. Noviss. Martii. Tom. II.

SAINT BRIDGET.

ST. BRIDGET saw some ducks swimming in a river, and sometimes flying in the air, so she called them to her. And the ducks, after a number of them had been collected, in obedience to the voice of the most holy virgin, came flying to her quite gently, without any fear. And the holy Mother for some time stroked them with her hand and embraced them, and then allowed them to return to their place of abode.

Now, the holy Bridget, seeing that she regarded no work as degrading, unless it was sinful, patiently endured her tasks, carried them out with foresight, and finished them with credit. Thus, at a certain time, several men were hospitably entertained by her father, and Bridget was summoned to prepare food for them, and she did not hesitate to accomplish satisfactorily the order of him who issued the command. So she set the cauldron on the fire and filled it with water, and placed as many pieces of meat in it as she thought necessary. And while she was busily engaged in her labours, a dog, which had just had puppies, came to the virgin and asked for nourishment as well as it could. What did the pitiful virgin do? Did she provide food for the hungry beast? Now, the quantity and number of pieces of meat was well known to the step-mother. Did she therefore refuse to give

the food to the dog? But to refuse help to the
needy was only to act contrary to herself. For
she was always loving, always tenderhearted,
always gentle and kind, and always abounding
in pity, in that she not only showed compassion
for the needs of men, but also extended it to
the necessities of beasts. Hence, because she
regarded her inborn pity of higher value than a
cruelty which was foreign to her nature, and also
having greater regard for a hungry beast than
for the mad rage of her step-mother, she bestowed
portions of the above-mentioned pieces of meat
on the hungry animal, for she had nothing
else at hand. It came a second time in like
manner, and found the virgin as disposed to
welcome it, as on the former occasion. And
just as a honeycomb overflowing with honey
gives forth a very sweet liquid, so the virgin,
too, being filled with natural affectionateness,
was easily influenced by the need of it. And
when afterwards her father sat down to supper
with his guests he bade them place on the table
the dish of boiled meat. So the virgin did as
her father ordered; for, trusting in God, she set
the pieces of meat before the guests, and they
were found to have increased both in size and
number, just as much as they had before been
diminished by her mercifulness.

Acta Sanct.; Ed. Noviss. Februarii. Tom. I.

SAINT KIERAN,

Patron of the Diocese of Ossory.

ONE day, by the help of God, St. Kieran made a beginning of his miracles in the Island of Clera, in the following manner: When he was a boy, a kite flew down from the sky and seized a bird sitting in its nest before the Saint, and carried it up in the sky in its talons. And when the blessed boy saw it he was much distressed at the pitiful sight, and prayed for the captive. Whereupon, the ravenous kite at once returned with the bird, and laid it before him, half-dead and wounded. And the wretched bird was healed by the grace of God before the eyes of this most dutiful boy, as he had desired in his heart, and proceeded to sit joyfully on its nest in safety.

When St. Kieran arrived there, he used at first to sit under a tree beneath the shade of which lived a very savage boar. When the boar first caught sight of a human being, it was frightened, and fled; but it was tamed by God, and returned like a friend—or, rather, a servant—to the man of God; and that boar became St. Kieran's first disciple in that place, as though it were a monk. For this same boar, before the eyes of the man of God, tore up with its strong teeth branches and grass for building the cell. Now, there was no one with the Saint of God at that time, because he had left his disciples and escaped alone to that desert. Afterwards other animals came from their hiding-places in the wilderness to St. Kieran—that is to say, a fox and a badger, a wolf and a stag—and stayed with him like tame animals, and obeyed him in his commands in all things, as if they were monks. Another day, a fox, which was more sly and crafty than other animals, stole some figs belonging to its Abbot, St. Kieran, and, giving up its good resolutions, it took them off to its former home in the desert, to eat them there. But when the holy Father knew this, he sent another "monk" or "disciple"—that is, Brother Badger—into the desert to bring Brother Fox back to his place; and, because Brother Badger was well used to woods, he hastened to obey his master's orders, and came straight to the cave of Brother Fox; and, finding him as he was on the point of eating his master's figs, he cut off his two ears and tail, and plucked off his hair, and made him accompany him to the monastery to do penance for his theft. So the fox and badger arrived at St. Kieran's cell at 3 o'clock, with the figs uninjured. Thereupon, the holy man says to Brother Fox, "Why have you, brother, committed this sin, which ill becomes a monk? Our water is good, and open to all; and our food, in like manner, is shared equally amongst us all; and, if you wanted to eat flesh, as you are accustomed to do, Almighty God would have made it for us from the bark of trees." Then Brother Fox begged for pardon, and repented with fasting, and touched no food till the Saint told him. After that it stayed on as one of the family with the rest. Then his disciples and many others came from all quarters to St. Kieran at the same place, and there they began to build the celebrated monastery. But the aforementioned tame animals were there during his lifetime, because holy St. Kieran liked much to see them in his old age.

Acta Sanct. Vet. et Majoris Scotiæ, sive Hiberniæ. Per R. P. F. J. Colganum. Tom I.

SAINT BERACH,

Abbot and Bishop in Spain.

ONCE, when the herdsman of the monastery was less watchful than usual over the flocks entrusted to his care, a wolf from a neighbouring spot, which was on the look-out for food, rushed out suddenly and killed the calf of a cow with an abundant supply of milk, and carried it off and ate it. Then its mother set up a terrible bellowing, and rushed about here and there as if it was mad. But the man of God prayed, and a wonderful thing happened. For the wolf ceased to be savage, and returned to the lowing cow as mild as a calf; and the cow licked it, and gave it an abundant supply of milk. And so it happened, by the grace of God, that the savage nature of the wolf was changed into the gentleness of the calf, so that in future it treated the cow no longer as a wolf, but as a calf.

Acta Sanct.; Ed. Noviss. Feb. Tom. II.

SAINT AIDAN,

Bishop and Patron of Ferns.

ONCE, when St. Aidan was staying in a solitary place, and was reading, a weary stag, pursued by dogs, came to him, and stood before the servant of God as if asking for protection; and he, understanding the reason of it, placed a cloth on its horns; and, when the dogs came after it, it looked to them a sort of ghost. And when the dogs were unable to find it there, they returned home. Thereupon the stag took off the cloth from its horns, and escaped free.

St. Aidan once came to a monastery called Seanbothai, near the foot of a mountain called in Gaelic Suighe Lagen; and, on the way, a she-wolf, panting exceedingly, and hungry, came in a friendly manner to him; and when the man of

God saw it, he said to the boy who stood near him, "Have you any food?" And the boy, not knowing what the Saint wanted, replied, "I have a loaf and part of a fish." Then the man of God took them, and gave them to the wolf; but the boy blushed and said, "I am afraid of my master." Then he said to him, "Bring me some leaves." And, when the leaves were brought, the man of God blessed them; and, by the grace of God, they were turned to use as food; so he handed them to the boy, and gave thanks to God.

SAINT PHARAÏLDE.

IN order that the extent of the Divine power might be made manifest, God, out of the depth of his kindness, condescended to work an extraordinary and memorable miracle on account of her deserts. When during the winter she visited a field, with slow and anile steps, where she had sown wheat, she found some birds gathered, which some call one name, some another, but which are commonly called geese. She drove them home with a stick like tame cattle; and when they got there, she shut them up in a fold like a flock of sheep, and she allowed none of them to be injured or killed, but kept them safe against the morrow. But one of her retainers went up to the monastery in the morning or evening, without her knowing it, and killed one of the above-mentioned birds, and ate it up with some friends of the same family. But when Pharaïlde, the Virgin of the Lord, returned from the monastery, she remembered the birds, and allowed none of them to be slaughtered, and permitted all to go away uninjured from the fold where she had penned them in. And when they were being released, and were walking off like geese or chicken, with bold steps, the blessed virgin knew that one was missing, either from one companion seeking another, or from the number being short of what it was, or else by Divine warning. And when she had searched carefully and earnestly where it had gone, and tried to find out whither it had fled, and the boy of the same house informed her, she learnt that it had been killed and eaten. To cut the story short, she ordered the bird's bones and feathers which could be found to be brought to her, and, by a stupendous miracle, put them together again, and revived the bird, and dismissed it to its usual feeding-grounds.

Acta Sanct.; Ed. Noviss. Januarii. Tom. I.

SAINT GUDWAL.

WE have been speaking hitherto about the wonderful works of God conspicuous in the miracles of Gudwal, which are not only to be wondered at in the four elements, not only confined to the souls and bodies of men, but also to be witnessed with pleasure amongst animals and beasts. And amongst these we now set before you what we have ascertained about a sheep, and the taming of wolves, and their transformation into creatures gifted, as it were, with reason. There were sheepfolds for the use of the monastery, which were much harassed by the attacks of wolves. Thence it happened one day that the shepherd laid at the Saint's feet a dead lamb which had been all but snatched from the very jaws of the wolf. Over the lifeless body the man of God turned to the Lord, and remindng himself of Christ, who was led as a sheep to the slaughter, and as a lamb before its shearers was dumb, he said: "Let my prayers come before Thee; incline Thine ear to my prayer, O Lord. Thou, Lord, in the person of David, thy servant, when breaking the mouths of lions and dashing in pieces the limbs of bears, didst deliver a lost sheep from the hand of death, and as the Good Shepherd thou didst seek and find it, leaving the ninety and nine in the wilderness, and didst place it on Thy shoulders, and bring it back to the flock; be mindful of these mercies, who encouragest our prayers, and show Thy kindness to this sheep, that, by raising it to life again thy great excellence may be made known which is extended to other creatures through our hands. Know, therefore, O Lord, that we are moved to these prayers more for Thy praise and for the glory of Thy Name than for any desire of earthly gain." He finished his prayer and touched the sheep's head with the top of the shepherd's staff while all were giving glory to God, and roused it with a gentle touch. And immediately it stood on its feet, and returned to its flock, to the no small amazement of many.

Again, he turned to God, and said: "Be pleased, O Lord, to bid the murderous invader of our flock to approach, that, by Thy favour, we may deal with him." When he had spoken thus, the wolf drew near more gently than a quiet dog, covered with the blood of its recent victim, as if it were aware of its fault, making satisfaction to the holy man, and throwing itself at his feet on the ground. Whereupon all present who saw it gave praise to God, and raised their hands in thanksgiving. But the holy Bishop rejoiced in the Lord, and said: "Begone, cruel beast, begone, and dare not from henceforth to disturb our sheep with any harm." It therefore gently withdrew at the Saint's command and changed its ways to the sheep by doing away with all cruelty, to which their nature so savagely stirs wild beasts. And so it turned out that, after this, as if fulfilling the duty of a shepherd, it so thoroughly looked after the welfare of the flock that it growled and gnashed its teeth, and forcibly attacked and drove away wolves and savage beasts, who approached the flock thirsting for blood.

At another time Saint Gudwal saw a wolf in the fields unable either to walk or run, rather dragging along the burden of its weak body than carrying it. And he, out of pity for its distress, cried out with a loud voice: "Inhabitant of the woods, who plottest against the innocence of unwary flocks, what misfortune has befallen thee that thy wonted swiftness has left thee, and an unnatural slowness takes its place?" At this address of the Saint the brute beast was endowed with sufficient reason, for by God's Providence it understood that it was to be the means of proclaiming the name of God amongst Christian people. Therefore it drew near with what strength it could, and bowed its head out of respect to him, and demonstrated its affection for him by bending its neck. It then proceeded to show him the claw of its foot, which was pierced by a thorn, and, as it were, began to pray him, as well as it could by the motion of its head, to apply the means for its recovery. But the man of God was struck with the display of so great intelligence in a heart without feeling, and gave praise to God and thanked him. He then stretched forth the pastoral staff, with which he had raised to life the dead sheep, and lightly touched the beast's lame foot, saying to God: "Thou, Lord, shalt save both man and beast." At these words a heavenly healing was placed in the hands of the man of God, just as with God Himself, and descended down the dry staff into the lame foot, the same as that with which the rod of Moses in Egypt was endued, for the purpose of working signs and wonders.

What marvellous sanctity! What mighty power the servants of God possess! how rich in miracles, and how active in healing! Then the Saint addressed the beast which was healed: "From henceforth, injure no creature more, but all thy days eat grass like an ox; make use of grass, I say, satisfy thy hunger with pulse, and so, in maintaining an innocent disposition, endeavour to pay the common debt of death." And there were many who saw the beast from that time become quite gentle, and give proof of its evident obedience to the Saint's commands.

Acta Sanct.; Ed. Noviss. Junii. Tom. I.

SAINT BALDOMAR.

IN the monastery of Saint Justin, Saint Baldomar chose a poor cell to dwell in, and while he occupied it, God of His mercy bestowed upon him such marks of his favour, that the birds of the air which had been caught or made prisoner by no man, came daily to take food from his hand, at the usual hour of meals; and when the man of God had fed them, he gave them the following advice : "Refresh yourselves with food, and always give thanks to the God of heaven."

Acta Sanct.; Ed. Noviss. Februarii. Tom. III.

SAINT WEREBURG.

GREATER than miracles are merits through which miracles take place. It is possible to have perfect merits without miracles, but miracles are nothing without merits. However, this most worthy Virgin was celebrated for many miracles, both in her home and wherever she lived. But in Weduna, her royal estate, which is situated in the province of Hampton, this pleasing miracle of hers, and one which will be held most remarkable from generation to generation, is vouched for by the whole people.

While the Virgin princess was living in the palace of Weduna a numerous flock of wild geese used to ravage her fields. And a labourer of her estate reported this damage to his mistress. Therefore, with wonderful faith, she ordered him to bring to her all the birds which devoured crops not belonging to them, and to shut them up like cattle. "Go," she said, "and bring hither all these birds." So he departed, in profound astonishment as to whether this order was mere idle talk or the words of a madwoman. For how could he imagine himself to be able to force so many winged strangers, who could escape through the sky, to walk on foot into captivity? "How," said he, "can I turn them hither? They will fly into the air at my first approach." Then the Virgin urging him on to do her commands, "Go," she said, "as quickly as you can, and, as we commanded you, bring all of them captive." He was afraid to neglect even what seemed to him a foolish order of his holy mistress; so he went after them and said: "Go quickly to our mistress"; and he drove them all before him like tame cattle. Now no bird out of that vast assembly lifted its wings, but like unfledged chickens, or those which have had their wings cut off, they advanced on their feet, walking with their necks bent down, as if out of shame for their guilt. And so they assembled in the court of their judge, trembling and subdued as if condemned, and there they were kept as captives, or, rather, were preserved for pardon. The daughter of light spent that night with sacred hymns and prayers, as was her custom. In the morning, however, all the strange birds uplifted their voices, and cried to the Lord as if they were asking for pardon and permission to depart. But she, seeing she was very kind to every creature of God, ordered them to be liberated and sent away, and cautioned them not to dare to return to this place. But one of the servants went out and stole one of them and hid it; and when they mounted up into the air with uplifted wing, and looked around and examined their flock, they perceived the loss to their company through the absence of one of them. Forthwith the whole crowd assembled over the house of the Virgin, and complained of the loss of their comrade with great clamour; the sky was covered on all sides with their scattered forces, so that they appeared to be laying their cause before their pitying judge as though to say: "What is the reason, Lady, that one of us is kept prisoner, when out of the kindness of your heart you have given us all our freedom? Is it possible that such a wrong can hide in your holy house, and that disgraceful robbery can flourish beneath your harmlessness?" Accordingly, the holy Virgin went out at this cry and complaint of this crowd of birds, and understood the reason for it, just as if she actually heard those words. Thereupon the guilty one openly confessed the detected robbery, and the holy peace-maker received the bird from his hands, and restored it to its fellows, bidding them to depart under the conditions above mentioned. At which she was so filled with joy that she said in her kind heart: "Bless the Lord, ye birds of the air." And immediately all that flock flew away, and no bird of this kind was ever found again in the land of the blessed Wereburg, as the wonderful story goes. Nobly, therefore, did these creatures obey her, who with heart and soul gave heed to the Creator of all things.

Acta Sanct.; Ed. Noviss. Februarii. Tom. I.

ST. ALDEMAR.

At one time, St. Aldemar happened to set out for a certain monastery which was named in honour of the Holy Mother of God, where he was long detained with the Brothers of that house by severe illness. However, at length the boon of health was restored to him, so he made his way back to the monastery over which he presided, where he had left a certain chest, which an immense number of bees had entered in a huge swarm by the keyhole, and had made there of honey no small store, and an enormous honey-comb. On his return thither after a few days, the bold Confessor opened the chest, which, as I remarked above, was locked, and ascertained what was concealed within. But the holy man was unwilling to disturb the bees; accordingly, he quickly left them, so as not to deprive them of the home they had chosen. What a wonderful loving-kindness the great man possessed! What a praiseworthy example for the imitation of all the faithful! How great love do you think he, who was so careful not to disturb unreasoning creatures, must have shown to man?

Acta Sanct.; Ed. Noviss. Mart. Tom. III.

SAINT NORBERT,

Founder of the Premonstratensians.

WHEN some Brothers had gone into the forest to cut wood, they discovered a wolf eating a wild buck. So they shouted out and chased it away, and took the prey which the rapacious wolf had seized, and carried it home with them, and hung it up in a corner, suspecting no harm. But the wolf, as if complaining of the wrong done to it, followed them, and sat down before the entrance to the house like a house-dog, and seemed to search for what had been taken from it. Now, those who came to the house without knowing what had happened, shouted at it, as usual, to drive it away ; but it looked at them in a friendly manner, and did not move. And when this was reported to the man of God, he assembled all the Brothers and enquired what it meant, and declared that so fierce an animal would not have assumed such a mild air without reason. But the Brothers who were aware of the reason, because they were afraid came forward openly and asked pardon for their fault, as if it were a serious one, and told what had taken place, and the wrong they thought they had done to the wolf. And when the man of God heard it, he said, "Give back what belongs to him, for you have acted unfairly in taking what was not yours." At last the wolf got back its prey, and departed to its home without injuring anyone.

It is well known, however, that on another day, a Brother, who was a cleric, had been sent to look after cattle in a field, and the wolf stood near them during the whole day while he was there; and, as if affording companionship for their keeper, it exhibited no signs of savageness. And when, as evening drew near, it was time for the flock to be led to their fold, the Brother on one side and the wolf on the other drove them in. But when the flock was brought home, and the Brother had shut the door, and left the wolf outside, it knocked at the door with its foot as well as it could, as if it was complaining of the slight shown to it, and was asking for the reward due to its services. So it knocked repeatedly, and showed that it wanted to enter and obtain a bit of food. But when the man of God heard of it, he said, "Why do you not open the door for a guest who knocks?" And when they answered that it was not a guest who was knocking, but a wolf which showed great persistency and would not go away for any of them, he called the Brothers and enquired of them how it came to be present there. And when all held their tongues, the cleric whom he had sent out in the morning to tend the flock was summoned, and enquiries were made from him as to who it was who had assisted him in guarding the flock. But he was afraid to mention what had happened to him; and yet, not daring to conceal his answer to the enquiries, he said, "That beast which is knocking at the door was with me to-day, and with me guarded the flock under my charge until they were shut up in their fold, as if they had been entrusted to its care." But when the man of God heard it, he said, "Give him some food, for he asks a reward for the service he has rendered; for the labourer is worthy of his hire."

SAINT GEORGE OF SUELLI.

THE loving kindness and pity possessed by this holy man was extended not only to men but to the birds which fly in the air. Sparrows, parched with thirst, used to pant in this dry place, without any hope of cooling their tongues; for that spot is utterly devoid of water. So he struck a rock with his staff, and such an abundant spring flowed out, that it neither increased with floods of rain, nor was diminished by the burning rays of the sun: because the Lord greatly loved this Saint.

Acta Sanct.; Ed. Noviss. Aprilis. Tom. III.

SANCTUARY FOR ANIMALS.

IN a remote district of Ulster are certain hills, on which cranes and other birds build their nests freely during the proper season. The inhabitants of that place allow not only men but even cattle and birds to be quiet and undisturbed, out of reverence for the holy Beanus, whose Church makes the spot famous. That renowned Saint, in a wonderful and strange manner, used to take care not only of birds but of their eggs.

In the South of Mornonia, between the hill of Brendan and the open sea which washes the coast of Spain and Ireland, is a large district which is shut in on one side by a river full of fish, and on the other by a small stream. And, out of reverence for the holy Brendan and other Saints of that locality, this affords a wonderful place of refuge, not only for men and cattle, but also for wild beasts, whether these are strangers or those which inhabit the district. Consequently stags, wild boars, hares, and other wild beasts, when they perceive that they can by no means escape from the dogs pursuing them, make their way as quickly as they can from remote parts to that spot. And when they have crossed the stream, they are at once safe from all danger; for the dogs in hunting are there brought to a standstill and unable to follow any further. How wonderful is the power of God! because, through the merits of the Saints, neither a greedy nature, nor a huntsman pressing on, nor the prey running before him, can lead wicked and persistent robbers to seize the booty within reach. In those two places of refuge the birds and beasts do not fly from human intercourse, owing to a long enjoyment of undisturbed peace, such as one meets with in a home.

Giraldi Cambrensis Opera. Ed. by J. F. Dimock, M.A. Vol. V. London, 1867. *Topographia Hibernica.*

SAINT HUGH OF LINCOLN.

This man, who had given himself up to God, striving to make greater progress day by day, showed himself so simple and kindly in all things that he tamed small birds and wood mice, popularly called "squirrels," and made them so familiar and gentle that they were wont to come out from the wood, noting his daily hour of supper, and he had them habitually with him at table in his cell; and they used to eat, not only at table but at his own dish and hand. For the very inhabitants of the woods, in a way, were sensible of his inborn kindness of heart and freedom from guile. Consequently they were not afraid to be amiable with such a single-hearted and inoffensive man.

But amongst other numerous proofs of his most holy life we do not think we ought to be silent about the fact that he used to keep a little bird, "Brownie," which was so tame and gentle that she came daily to his table, as if she had discovered the inborn kindness of the man, to take food and meat there from his hand and plate. And this every day of the year, except only during nesting time. For during the whole of that time she was absent, and gave full play to her natural instincts. But she who had left him, as if to make compensation for her long absence, returned at the proper time with her family, and came, as she had been accustomed, to his table, and presented her young ones, now fledged and full grown, to her master. And this very pleasing and wonderful episode lasted for the kind man three whole years, until, in the fourth year, the bird, by some accident, as was supposed, died and ceased her visits, to the great grief of the amiable Saint.

Giraldi Cam. Op. Ed. J. F. Dimock, M.A. Vol. VII. Vita S. Hugonis.

BLESSED TORELLO OF POPPI.

A CERTAIN Count Charles, of Poppi, a friend of Blessed Torello, arriving late on Quinquagesima Sunday, sent him his squire with a basket filled with meat and bread; and as the squire was on his way, the ladies of Poppi gave him some luxuries to carry to the Brother. He therefore presented what had been given to him, and Torello graciously accepted it, and returned the empty basket to the young man, who wondered how he alone could consume so much in one evening. So he said to Torello: "How is it that you can eat so much, seeing you live alone?" "It is true," he replied, "that I live alone; but a friend of mine, who has a large appetite, will be here directly, for he has only gone out into the wood. Return, my son, before it gets late." So the young man took the basket and pretended to go away, but hid himself in a wood near the door, saying to himself: "I shall see from here if he is waiting for a friend," for he wanted to know who it was. Meanwhile Torello prayed to God, asking that his friend might approach. And as he prayed a wolf drew near the door with its mouth open and howling. So Torello opened the door and gave it the meat which had been brought to him. And after the wolf had eaten it up it began to fawn upon him, and placed its feet upon his breast, and licked the Brother like a dog, on account of his holiness, and as if it would ask for more. And Torello said to it: "Depart, my brother, and return to the wood, and there I command, in the name of Christ, that henceforth neither you, nor any other wolf, dare to injure any one of Poppi or of its neighbourhood, at least as far as the bell of the Abbey can be heard." When the wolf heard this it bowed its head and went away. But the young man who had concealed himself to see what would follow departed in amazement, and told everyone what had taken place.

Acta Sanct.; Ed. Noviss. Martii. Tom. II.

SAINT GEROLD OF SAXONY.

THE sixth lesson of the Breviary of Einsiedeln informs us in the following words about Gerold, who was discovered in his retreat by Otto, a count of Jagberg. He had begun to build a small cell, in which he lived such a holy and harmless life, and in such want of necessaries that, as a reward, he was blessed not only with the appearance of angels, but also with their good services, inasmuch as he frequently received from them the necessaries of life. This brilliant lamp tried to hide its light under a bushel; but it was revealed unexpectedly to Otto, Count of Jagberg. Some huntsmen had informed Otto that a bear pursued by dogs had run to the feet of the Saint, and was immediately safe from the bite or bark of the dogs by means of the staff alone which he carried. Wherefore the Count ran and embraced him most warmly, and treated him with profound reverence, and gave him no small part of his domain in which to build a house for the people of God. And Gerold did this, and the bear assisted him, for he thereafter made use of it, as if it were a servant, to draw and carry wood and stones.

POPE PAUL II.

HE was so gentle and possessed of such tenderness of disposition that he would not suffer men to be killed, nor even living creatures of any other kind to be slaughtered or dragged to death in his presence. He never allowed chickens or other birds to be killed while he was looking on, and he went so far as to snatch many of them out of the hands of his servants, and let them go away alive and uninjured. From the windows of his house at Rome he once saw a certain butcher dragging a calf to the slaughter-house, so he ordered the butcher to be brought to him at once, and, having ascertained the price of the calf, he had him paid in full, and requested him to lead the calf as soon as possible to the herd and to let it live. Also, while passing through the city of Sutrina, he saw a she-goat in the hands of a butcher, which had been caught to be killed; so he made the butcher desist from his purpose, and forthwith paid him what he asked for it, and ordered the she-goat to be let go uninjured and allowed to live.

Pauli II. Veneti Pont. Max. Vita ex cod. Angelicæ Bibliothecæ descripta. Romæ, MDCCXL.

SAINT FRANCIS DE PAULA.

ONE day the good Father, whilst walking through a wood, found a young hind; and when some men tried to capture it, he forbade them to touch it, and he cut off a part of its ear. Some time afterwards it fled to the good Father's room because it was in danger of being caught, and from henceforth followed him wherever he went, even to the Church, licking his robes and fawning upon him as its defender, and was easily recognised from the tip of its ear having been cut.

Another time, when the cells of the Brothers of the Pauline Monastery were being built, the same Brothers were carrying stones; but in the place where the stones were drawn they found a wasp's nest, and the wasps flew out when the stones were moved and rushed at the Brothers with such a loud buzzing that they fled away to the good Father, who was then working as a mason, to tell him what had happened. Whereupon he himself came to the place where the wasps were, and ordered all the Brothers to go away, and in obedience to him they went; but I stood still at the entrance to see what he would do. And I saw that he collected all those wasps and carried them to a wood bordering on the Monastery, and they were never seen again afterwards.

Acta Sanct.; Ed. Noviss.

On the 18th day of July, Master Peter of Genoa said that, when a certain man had come from the district of Renva to Paula to Brother Francis, twelve miles off, and had brought him some fish tied by the neck, which had been caught in fresh water, and had presented them to Brother Francis, he said: "Do you see how we are keeping those poor things in captivity?" So he released them one by one from the string by which they were suspended, and put them in a vessel of water. And when they were placed there they began immediately to revive and to play about. And when the witness himself, and others standing near, had seen the miracle—namely, that dead fish came to life again—they began to weep for joy. This was about 40 years ago or thereabouts.

Processus Inform. ad Canoniz.; Processus Consentinus.

The noble Philip Coningham, a citizen of the (Royal) territory, asserted on oath and laying his hand on the Bible, as to the sort of man he knew Blessed Francis of Paula to be for 40 years, and how famed he was for his holy life; and he knew by report that he had wrought great miracles. Amongst others, he narrates the incident of the dead fish which were thrown into the piscina and brought to life again. Likewise he recalls that when some huntsmen had found a buck, and were pursuing it with dogs, it made its way, in its flight, to the cell of Francis for protection, and the dogs saw it there, but they did not dare advance any further to seize the animal, but rather retreated. And these wonderful things were done at the town of Paula forty years ago! . . .

Processus Calabricus.

———

The Saint brought up a little lamb so tame that it followed him and fawned upon him like a puppy. Now, some labourers, urged on by the desire for meat to eat, killed and cooked it, and did away with all traces of it, so that they threw its skin, together with its bones, into a burning lime-kiln, lest they should betray the theft. They could not, however, hide it from some of the Brothers, and as they told the Saint about it he pretended not to believe them, and replied that the lamb would come if it was called. So he arrived at the lime-kiln and called out "Martinella!"—for this was the name he had given the lamb—and it responded with the usual bleating, and came forth alive from the fire, to the amazement of all. . . .

———

Moreover, God wrought a more astonishing miracle in the spring already mentioned; for, when the Saint threw into it a dead trout which had been given to him, it suddenly became alive, and afterwards became so tame that it readily swam to him in answer to its name, Antonella, and allowed him to stroke its back with his hand while eating the crumbs thrown to it. Now, a

Priest, Paulanus by name, easily caught it while eating crumbs thrown into the water, and prepared it for his supper. And when the holy Father became acquainted with it, for God revealed the thief to him, he sent one of his religious to the Priest to ask for the fish in his name. But the Priest returned an uncourteous answer, and denied what he had done. The messenger was sent a second time, and was ordered to say that the fish had just been cooked for supper; and that, if the Priest did not send it, evil would befall him. So touched was the Priest at being found out that, when brought before the Brother, he threw himself at his feet and bade him punish him in any way he pleased. Under the circumstances, it could not happen otherwise than that the fish should fall to pieces upon coming from the fire; so the Brother picked them up from the ground and brought them to Francis. And he addressed it as if it was alive: "Antonella, how badly you must have been treated for you to approach in this manner; this is the result of a greedy appetite, for this would never have happened to you if you had not greedily devoured the crumbs thrown to you by the Priest. Now, be more cautious after this experience, and in the name of the Lord receive your life back again." At these words the pieces were thrown into the water, and they came together and were restored to life, and remained so as long as the Saint lived. But when the news of his death was brought from France, and the trout was not seen any more, it was discovered that it appeared to have died the same day as the Saint did. The Priest, however, when he was aware of the miracle that had taken place, repented of his theft, and, on seeking pardon, he heard nothing more bitter from the smiling Saint than this: that the property of another is never any good to him who has obtained it wrongfully.

THE VEN. JOSEPH OF ANCHIETA.

He was accustomed to visit certain villages. Now panthers live in the colony of January, and in the mountains which extend to the cold extremity of the range, and come down to the sea shore. And while he was passing through this district with his attendants, and the others, overtaken by darkness, had built a hut for themselves (as they usually did), and rested their bodies, the Father, as his custom was, left the hut in the silence of the night to commune with God, and returned after some time bringing bunches or clusters of the fruit of that district, called bananas; and he threw them out and said in the Brazilian language: "Take your meal, my children." And on a brother enquiring who his friends were to whom he had thrown bananas during the night, he replied, "Some companions of mine." When it was morning the footprints of two panthers were seen on the ground, which had been close to him during the night while he was engaged in prayer, and, when he had finished, had followed him on his return to the hut. For, by a divine instinct, according to their power of discernment, they loved the man, whom, like other animals who loved him, they felt to be free from all human guile, and beloved of God Himself.

As he was journeying with some of the inhabitants, they came across a viper by the way (this kind of snake possesses a deadlier venom than any known in Europe); and when his companions saw it they fled from it in terror. But the Father called them back, and ordered the viper to come to him, and it obeyed. Whereupon he sat down and took it up and placed it in his lap, and, stroking it gently with his hand, embraced the opportunity of telling them much about the divine power, and pointing out that no created thing will refuse to recognise man's authority, so long as it is in no way contrary to God's laws. Having concluded his lengthy remarks on this subject, he earnestly encouraged the inhabitants to obey the laws of Christ, and then he gently dismissed the viper with his blessing. And he met a second viper on another journey, from which his companion ran away in alarm; and, though the Father called him back, he continued to run. Then the Father placed his foot upon it, as if mocking it, and encouraged it to bite him, and avenge the slights put upon its anger. But it raised its neck, and turned its head from side to side without doing any injury. And he so impressed his companion with his trust in God, as to cause him to fix his thoughts on God: and then he let the viper go,

ST. JEROME COMPANIONED BY ANIMALS.
(*Albert Dürer.*) See p. viii.

in the same manner as the former one, with the caution that it should injure no man.

It is commonly reported of Joseph that when he travelled he was wont to stretch out his arm and call birds to him, and bid them sit on his finger and praise God; and the birds used to obey him; and when they had sung a long time, as if they had accomplished their task, he sent them away and said to them : "When you have sufficiently praised God, go in peace." Swallows did the same, as he looked out of the window of his room, in the house of the Holy Spirit. These and other things in his life have been commonly noted by the Father and Brothers while he was at the head of the Society of Jesus, in the prefecture of the Holy Ghost.

As some men were on their return from fishing, and were wending their way to Saint Barnabas, one of the fishermen pierced with an arrow a large bearded ape (which is common in these parts) sitting on a tree; and when it fell the whole crowd of apes set up a loud cry, as at the death of their father, and ran to it with great alarm. Then the fishermen began to kill them also for food: for the Brazilians are as fond of eating them as other nations are of birds, pigs, and hares. For it is not to be wondered at that men who regard human flesh as the greatest delicacy should not shrink from eating an animal which resembles the human race in body. However, the Father forbade the fishers to kill such animals as these, and ordered them only to seek for amusement from such laughable creatures; and that he might afford the greater pleasure to the fishermen, he ordered the apes, in the Brazilian language, to attend to the funeral rites of their companion. Thereupon each of them hastened to obey him, and set up a great clamour and wailing; and some ran about on the ground and others leapt from branch to branch, and from tree to tree, and performed the funeral rites aloft, and upbraided their assailants for the unjust slaughter made in their flock, as far as they were able, with dismal cries and ridiculous grimaces. And so the wretched beasts, after having afforded pleasant sport to the enemies of their flock for the space of about three miles by this funeral display, approached the village. For fear they should be treated badly by the inhabitants, the Father ordered them to retire to their abode; and they took some provisions with them and retired to the woods.

Josephi Anchietæ. S. J., Sac. in Brasilia, Vita a S. Beretario, S. J., Lugduni, MDCXVII.

ST. ROSE OF LIMA.

A mark of honour—or, rather, of indulgence —was granted to Rose, while living in solitude, by gnats. Where the virgin's anchorite cell stood, the dampness of the soil and abundance of shrubs either produced a vast multitude of gnats, or drew them into its hospitable shade. There is no creature more annoying to man: for with its proboscis alone it acts the part of a trumpeter and soldier ; since it both stings with its proboscis, and by its shrill buzzing haunts the sleepers. Now, swarms and hosts of them used to enter Rose's hut, chiefly when either the parching rays of the sun by day, or at evening the calm, refreshing breezes of the night, brought their minute bodies down upon her. However, amidst such myriads of gnats, there was not one which ever touched Rose in her cell. The walls were full of them on all sides ; the little door resounded with them ; the window was crowded with a continuous stream of them coming and going ; but they all took care not to settle on Rose: as if by agreement they spared their hostess. Now, it happened that either the Mother or some of the more devout, by the confessor's permission, visited Rose in her narrow dwelling to discuss sacred topics. But an army of gnats attacked them as soon as they rested at the door or window, and their unwelcome numbers began at once to cover their faces and hands. One was driven away, it was followed by four; generally they lay in ambush to suck the blood of the careless, and left marks of their presence by irritation and swellings. They wondered how Rose could remain undisturbed for days together under this plague of Egypt; and they were more astounded when they observed that there was not the least trace on her face or hands of this bloodthirsty nuisance. Then the virgin smiled, and replied to the Mother and others: "When I entered this abode I made friends with the gnats, and formed a compact with them, that they should never disturb nor molest me, and that I, on my part, should in no way injure them. Each of us has stood to our agreement, and we not only enjoy this common dwelling without strife, but, moreover, the same gnats eagerly assist us, in their measure, in singing God's praises."

This was evidently the case. For as often as Rose at early dawn opened the door of her house, and undid the shutters of her windows, she charged the gnats (as many as had passed the night in crowds on the walls), "Come, now, my friends, it is time to praise Almighty God." And forthwith they, beginning with a gentle symphony, burst out into deep buzzing, and broke up into circles, mingling their high-pitched murmurs in various keys, in such ordered array and in such fitly-winding curves, that you would have thought it was either a chorus or dance, presided over by reason as conductor. When they had fulfilled this duty, they flew away to get food. And again, in like manner, when at sunset they returned to the hospitable roof, again Rose pressed on them the duty of joining with her for a certain space in giving praise to their common Creator before they retired to rest. Soon a joyful buzzing, in which they vied with one another, filled the corners of the room, and the winged harmony exulted in imitating the strains of wind instruments until, at Rose's orders, all at once were still, as if under the single rule of silence after dark. And this great authority over the lowest of animals she kept up by her harmless ways, which she developed in such a degree that she lived in her solitary cell as if she were in paradise. Sister Catharine of St. Mary, belonging to the third Order of St. Dominic, and Eleanor of Castro, an aged companion, used to visit Rose in her desert; but, because she was not able to put up with the importunity of the gnats, with her hand Catharine killed one filled with blood. But Rose, like one in amazement, said, "Do you venture to kill my guests?" But Catharine replied, "Say enemies, rather than guests,* for see how full this gnat is of my blood." And Rose remarked, "Is it a great matter that a tiny insect like that should feed on our blood, when its Creator so often feeds us with His own blood? Do not, therefore, continue to kill my gnats, and I, on my part, promise you that they shall keep the peace with you, as they do with me." And so it turned out; for no gnat after that molested Catharine.

In the last year of Rose's life, during the whole of Lent a little bird with a wonderfully strong, sweet voice used to fly opposite Rose's chamber at sunset, and perch on a neighbouring

* A play on the words "hostes" (enemies) and "hospites" (guests).

tree facing it, as if it was ready at a given signal to burst into song. When Rose saw her evening flute-player, she got ready herself to sing praise to God. Then, as if the signal were given, she invited the bird to join in her tune which she had composed for the purpose, that they might make harmony.

Rose's extreme gentleness and tender pity embraced brute beasts, since, as Solomon testifies, Proverbs xii. : "The upright knows the souls of his own beasts of burden, but the heart of the wicked is cruel." Mary of Oliva had in her chicken-yard a wonderfully beautiful young cock. On its back and wings were brightly interwoven variegated colours and a pleasing motley of striped feathers. Its neck was ringed with a purple collar, and its body, with the graceful arch of its tail feathers, seemed to end in the colours of the rainbow. In short, this handsome beast was a delight to the whole household, and all rejoiced that it was being brought up and kept by the lady of the house in hopes of rearing some descendants which would take after it. The young one grew, but it was so slothful in its fat body that it continually sat on the ground, and was hardly ever seen to rise on its feet, and was never heard to crow. The lady of the house was displeased with it, because she thought it was hopeless to expect any offspring from such a sire; so she made up her mind, as she sat at table with her husband and sons, to kill this unprofitable cockerel the same evening, and to serve it up next day for dinner.

The young Rose, as she stood there, pitied the bird, and, in her unaffected innocence, turned to it like a child and said: "Crow, my chick, crow, or you will die." The girl had hardly spoken these words when, before the eyes of all, the fowl suddenly rose to its feet and vigorously flapped its wings and crowed melodiously and merrily. It next proceeded to walk, with high and proud steps, about the whole yard, and crowed readily several times, with extended breast, when Rose bade it. Those who were present laughed at the sentence of death having been suddenly recalled, and the fowl flapped its wings and crowed repeatedly in company with them as they clapped their hands, and strutted about as if magnificently clad. And, with extended neck, the noisy bird started afresh the laughter of the inmates as they applauded. From that time it often by day filled the neighbourhood with its tuneful note. The household counted the number of times, and found it crowed occasionally fifteen times in the short space of a quarter of an hour. Moreover, the lady of the house was not disappointed of her hopes, for shortly afterwards this bird became the sire of some very handsome chickens. So far did the words of the compassionate Rose prevail to save the life of a brute beast.

Acta Sanct.; Ed. Noviss. Aug. Tom V.

A Cloud of Witnesses.

The Being that is in the clouds and air,
  That is in the green leaves among the groves,
Maintains a deep and reverential care
  For the unoffending creatures whom He loves.

WORDSWORTH.

A Cloud of Witnesses.

CARDINAL MANNING.

AN Anti-Vivisection annual meeting was held in the drawing-room of the Lord Chief Justice of England in Sussex Square, the chair being taken by the Earl of Shaftesbury.

CARDINAL MANNING said: I shall scrupulously follow the example of our chairman by saying only a very few words. Meeting here to-day, in the house of the Lord Chief Justice, we have very high sanction for our work. We should not have met here if a very wise head, full of deliberation, had not given our object his sanction. So far, then, we are not likely to be challenged either on points of law or wisdom. Being here to-day, the duty that falls upon me is to propose: "That the transactions, No. 2 of the Victoria Street Society, be adopted as the report of the Society."

I am very glad to move this resolution, for in two years I have not had the opportunity of expressing what I feel on this subject. There are men present now who know that before that period I was slow in expressing strongly what I feel and desire. Then conviction had not been awakened; and I take the first opportunity that has been offered me to renew publicly my firm determination, so long as life is granted to me, to assist in putting an end to that which I believe to be a detestable practice, without scientific results, and immoral in itself (cheers), believing as I do, that it cannot be controlled, though we have endeavoured to control it. We have had a most elaborate commission and report, laying down a number of conditions under which this practice must be admitted, legislation was founded on that report, and I believe that not only has that legislation been ineffectual, but that we have been entirely hoodwinked, and the law has not been carried into effect. I believe the time has come, and I only wish that we had the power legally to prohibit altogether the practice of vivisection (applause). I am quite prepared then to adopt the report in my hand, and I do so for reasons which I find in the report itself, which I read through attentively and carefully this morning. One reason why I am glad to adopt the report is contained in the memorial to Mr. Gladstone (page 25) where I read: "The Act, 39 and 40 Vic. c. 77, which promised to effect the reconciliation between the claims of science and humanity, has proved so ineffectual that some of the experiments cited as typically cruel before the Royal Commission (notably Dr. Rutherford's) have been in 1878 repeated under the direct sanction of the law; while three times as many vivisectors were licensed in 1878 as there were men engaged in such pursuits throughout the kingdom in 1875." That passage, I think, was written after careful and exact examination of the facts, all abundantly proving what is asserted, viz., that the statute that was passed two years ago has been ineffectual, and that, as we cannot control, we must prohibit (cheers). I read also, in the same document, that Dr. Lauder Brunton experimented on ninety cats, and Dr. Rutherford on forty dogs, all of whom endured many days of torture ; of cases of dogs and rabbits baked and stewed to death by Claude Bernard, and of twenty-five dogs covered with turpentine and roasted alive by Professor Wertheim ; and I only ask whether, in the name of "science," experiments of that kind can be permitted? The same document says, and says most wisely : " Let not the name of science be made odious by responsibility for deeds, which, if committed openly in our streets, would call forth the execrations of the roughest of the populace." Then, again : The history of the existing Act has shown it is futile to attempt to separate the use of vivisection (if lawful use it have) from abuse. Between sanctioning its atrocities and stopping the practice altogether there is no middle course. By prohibiting vivisection "you will at one and the same time save numberless animals from pangs which add no small item to the sum of misery upon earth, and men from acquiring that hardness of heart and deadness of conscience for which the most brilliant discovery of physiology would be poor compensation."

I think these sentences both weighty and true (hear, hear). I was not before aware of the horrors which had been perpetrated. In page 34 of the report there is a reference to the pamphlet on the "Action of Pain on Respiration," by the physiologist Mantegazza. The Professor describes the methods which he devised for producing pain. It seems they consisted in "planting nails, sharp and numerous, in such a manner as to render the creature almost motionless, because in every movement it would have felt its torment more acutely." Further on he mentions that, to produce still more intense pain, he was obliged to employ lesions, followed by inflammation. An ingenious machine constructed by "our" T—— of M——, enabled him likewise to grip any part of an animal with pincers with iron teeth, and to crush, to tear, to lift up the victim, "so as to produce pain in every possible way." The first series of his experiments, Signor Mantegazza informs us, were tried on twelve animals, chiefly rabbits and guinea pigs, of which several were pregnant. One poor little creature, "far advanced in pregnancy," was made to endure *dolori atrocissimi*, so that it was impossible to make any observations in consequence of its convulsions.

Nothing can justify—no claim of science, no conjectural result, no hoped-for discovery—such horrors as these. (Applause.) Also, it must be remembered, that, whereas these torments, refined and indescribable, are certain, the result is altogether conjectural—everything about the result is uncertain but the certain infraction of the first laws of mercy and humanity. (Loud applause.) But, on the other hand, I know that Sir William Fergusson, whom we have lately lost, has declared that science had never received the slightest augmentation from vivisection, and no man had greater experience than he; and I know that Sir Charles Bell, who with the practical knowledge of Fergusson, had a scientific genius peculiarly his own, has left a record that no gains to science have resulted from vivisection. Then, I say, we are misled, if we believe that vivisection leads us legitimately on the path of discovery (hear, hear.) I am firmly convinced that there is only one thing to do, and that is to make the statute law of the land stronger than it is. Let me believe that England is free from the enormities practised abroad. I love my country and my countrymen, but I will not confide in the notion that that which has been practised abroad, has not been, and cannot be, practised in our midst; and if I thought that there was at this moment a comparative exemption in England, I would say: "Let us take care that there shall never be re-action of the Continent on this country: for it is true and certain that whatever is done abroad, within a little while is done among ourselves, unless we render it impossible that it should be done."

One of the most interesting parts of this report is that which states that, "The young men of both the Universities had been engaging themselves on the subject, and that in the Oxford Union Debating Society, when the subject was discussed, the anti-vivisectionists carried the resolution." The opinions of the young men of the day are the prophecies of the future; and if we can educate our young men in an abhorrence of cruelty, practised in the name of science, your hands will be so strengthened that the day will not be far distant when you will be able to control this great evil. (Loud applause.)

"*The Zoophilist*," *London, July 1st*, 1881.

At a similar meeting a year later, CARDINAL MANNING moved a resolution: "That this meeting adopts Mr. Reid's Bill for the Total Abolition of Vivisection." His Eminence said: My Lord Shaftesbury—I think that if we are by these practices to reduce our medical men and surgeons, and those into whose hands we fall in moments of suffering, to a state of moral insensibility like this, then happy will be those who slip out of the world without passing through their hands. (Applause.) Well, then, it appears to me that, as we have the uncertainty of the result, and the certainty of atrocious and unimaginable suffering, we have a case so strong that I cannot understand any civilised man committing or countenancing the continuance of such a practice. An impression has been made that those whom I represent look, if not with approbation, at least with great indulgence, at the practice of vivisection. I grieve to say that abroad there are a great many (whom I beg to say I do not represent) who do favour this practice; but this I do protest, that there is not a religious instinct in nature, nor a religion of nature, nor is there a word in revelation, either in the Old Testament or in the New Testament, nor is there to be found in the great theology which I do represent, no, nor in any act of the Church of which I am a member; no, nor in the lives and utterances of any one of the great servants of that Church who stand as examples, nor is there an authoritative utterance anywhere to be found in favour of vivisection. There may be the chatter, the prating and the talk of those who know nothing about it. And I know what I have stated to be the fact; for, some years ago, I took a step, known to our excellent Secretary, and brought the subject under the notice and authority where alone I could bring it. And those before whom it was laid soon proved to have been profoundly ignorant of the alphabet even of vivisection. They believed entirely that the practice of surgery, and the science of anatomy, owed everything to the discoveries of vivisectors. They were filled to the full with every false impression; but when the facts were made known to them, they experienced a revulsion of feeling. I will only detain you further to ask—If vivisection is to be continued where is its term or limit to be? What is to be its limit if we are to be vivisectors not for utility but for science? (Hear, hear). And if we are to proceed upon the whole animal creation, multiplying experiments on every vein, every nerve, every muscle, every function of the body, with every drug to be applied, and every surgical instrument to be used, I would ask— Where is to be the end of such practice? To me, than this nothing more horrible can be conceived. I quite agree with what your Lordship said a year ago. I do not believe this to be the way that the All-Wise and All-Good Maker of us all has ordained for the discovery of the healing art which is one of His greatest gifts to men. He has, indeed, attached labour to the drawing of the harvest out of the soil; but I do not believe the revelation of the healing art will come in the furrow of the atrocious suffering which vivisection inflicts on animals. I cannot believe it. I cannot call it a truthful doctrine, but a superstition. But I leave it to the scientists, and if they believe it, then, in my opinion, they are the most superstitious men on earth. (Loud applause.)

I sincerely hope that these two Bills will pass into law, and that they will put a check on this most atrocious practice. (Renewed applause.)

"The Zoophilist," London, July 1st, 1882. *Annual Meeting of the Victoria Street Society for the Protection of Animals from Vivisection.*

The annual assembly of the members and friends of the Society for the Protection of Animals from Vivisection was held in 1884 at the Westminster Palace Hotel. Cardinal Manning, Archbishop of Westminster, presided.

HIS EMINENCE : — My Lord, Ladies, and Gentlemen,—Nobody denies the lawfulness of capital punishment, I believe, except certain theorists, who, happily, have not prevailed upon the intelligence of mankind. It is written in the Holy Writ, and we are not wiser than that Book; but who will tell me that the lawfulness of capital punishment justifies the infliction of torture? Your Lordship has just spoken of a proposition, made in the time of Charles II., that convicts whose lives were forfeited to the State might be operated upon by the infliction of surgical torture. Who would say that capital punishment includes the right to inflict torture? (Hear, hear.) Nobody, I believe, except certain very excellent people, whom I respect in their life, but not in their theology, maintains the unlawfulness of war. Well, no one maintains that, if war be lawful, the use of explosive bullets or of poisoned wells, or the infliction of any kind of cruelty is justified, and contained in the right to make war. Therefore, it is clear that the words "kill and eat," and the dominion which the beneficent Maker of all things has given to man over the lower creatures, do not justify the infliction of exquisite torment in the name of science—the most misleading of all the cries of the nineteenth century — nine-tenths of which is curiosity, issuing, I will not even say in knowledge, but issuing in a supposed knowledge which I believe to be in a large measure barren of result. (Applause.) Therefore, my Lord, I am most happy to move the adoption of this report.

Special Supplement to " The Zoophilist." London, July 1st 1884. Annual Meeting of the Victoria Street and International Society.

At a similar meeting in 1887, CARDINAL MANNING said: A literary man of great reputation and highly celebrated for his literary powers, but not equally so for his accuracy, I believe, was present at one of our meetings, and he heard out of my mouth this statement : That inasmuch as animals are not moral persons we owe them no duties, and that, therefore, the infliction of pain is contrary to no obligation. Now, he omitted to say that I did make that statement for the purpose only of refuting it. (Applause.) But he put it into my mouth, and there it is in a book that is sold at all the bookstalls in the railway stations, and I am credited to this day with that which I denounced as a hideous, and, I think, an absurd doctrine. (Hear, hear.) It is perfectly true that obligations and duties are between moral persons, and, therefore, the lower animals are not susceptible of those moral obligations which we owe to one another; but we owe a seven-fold obligation to the Creator of those animals. Our obligation and moral duty is to Him who made them, and if we wish to know the limit and the broad outline of our obligation, I say at once it is His nature and His perfections, and among those perfections one is most profoundly that of eternal mercy. (Hear, hear.) And, therefore, although a poor mule or a poor horse is not, indeed, a moral person, yet the Lord and Maker of that mule and of that horse is the highest Lawgiver, and His nature is a law to Himself. And, in giving a dominion over His creatures to man, He gave it subject to the condition that it should be used in conformity to His own perfections, which is His own law, and, therefore, our law. (Hear, hear.) It would seem to me that the practice of vivisection, as it is now known, and now exists, is at variance with those moral perfections.

"*The Zoophilist.*" *London, April 1st*, 1887.

ARCHBISHOP BAGSHAWE.

SPEAKING in 1903, at an Anti-Vivisection Conference, ARCHBISHOP BAGSHAWE said: I am sorry that I cannot agree with our Chairman's proposal, that there should be left certain centres in which vivisection should be carried on with the sanction of the State, for I think that the arguments of others, so ably put forward, as to the impossibility of providing any adequate supervision and preventing cruelty, are conclusive, inasmuch as those entrusted with the recommendation of such centres are vivisectors, and the higher they get in their profession, sometimes the most cruel vivisectors. We should have no sort of security against those evils continuing—perhaps in fewer centres, but still continuing in our midst, and handing down traditions of cruelty to succeeding generations. I think the discussion has been exceedingly interesting, and especially the papers that have been read showing that the vivisectors can prove nothing that has been gained to science by what they have done. They have really never made out a case for vivisection, and the admissions that we have read to-day show that they have no case; but whether they have or not, I think the objections to vivisection are extremely grave. In the first place, it leads to a good deal of error, as the vivisectors themselves have acknowledged. They come to no certain conclusions, because they examine the conditions of life under circumstances utterly disturbing to the ordinary processes of life. And, again, that which is natural to one animal is not necessarily natural to man. Indeed, they themselves are now often saying that vivisection upon animals is of little or no use; that nothing good will be gained until they vivisect men. I do think that that is a most fearful danger. (Hear, hear.) From what I have heard, I have no doubt that in some foreign hospitals, and, I fancy, a good deal quietly among ourselves, experiments are made of one kind or another on our poor patients, simply as experiments without reference to their good. If that is the case, it is a most awful thing, and that it will be the case, if scientific vivisection goes on and increases, I do not think anyone can possibly doubt. I hold that the danger of putting a weapon of this kind in the hands of those who have power over the poor in our hospitals far outweighs any possible gain that might be to science. There is another grievous danger in vivisection. It is now claimed that psychology is a part of physiology; that the science of mind is merely a department of the science of the human frame, with its germ cells, and other parts by which the action is developed; and that mind distinctly is the activity of those germ cells; that is to say, that mind proceeds from matter, and that matter can generate intelligence and will. Well, I think you will all see that this is a denial of the human soul, and would tend to a denial of Almighty God's action. If matter can develop into mind and will and intelligence, matter may have created the world. They certainly do claim, for the sentence I am referring to was very distinct, that, inasmuch as mind was the activity of an organism, therefore necessarily psychology or the science of mind was a mere department of physiology or the science of the body. To encourage such speculations is a most horrible evil. If doctors are to be turned from their proper position, and made to talk of these things of which they understand nothing, and confound sciences together in that absurd fashion—to say, that because they are good with the microscope, therefore they can teach us all about the intelligence and the mind— it is a very grievous evil, and, I suppose, absolutely destructive of Christianity. Another, and perhaps the worst evil of vivisection, is that it encourages that cruelty which is certainly one of the characteristics of fallen man, a passion which he likes to gratify as much as he likes to gratify other passions, and which easily grows to a monstrous extent if it is at all encouraged. When one reads the accounts written by vivisectors themselves of their spending day after day in torturing whole multitudes of animals with the most fearful torture, apparently with no direct object at all (because in by far the greater part of their experiments there is nothing to be proved, except to see the result of their torture and the pain that it inflicts), one cannot but shudder at the idea of such a fearful amount of cruelty being pandered to and allowed to grow in their hearts. Really, I feel that I could scarcely shake hands with, or acknowledge as a friend at all, a man who could deliberately spend his days in that kind of thing. (Cheers.) And I am quite sure, however much they may talk about their not forgetting the difference between man and other animals, that any man who takes a delight in vivisecting dogs all day long, would not hesitate very much at vivisecting men, if he got the chance of doing so without opprobrium. I do not hold exactly with the "rights" of animals. I have noticed a confusion in some of the speeches on this question between animals and man. Men have reason and free will, and it is necessary to have reason and free will in order to have a right, properly speaking, at all. That which is not intelligent has not a right. But, nevertheless, we have duties, though they have not rights. We have the duty to imitate the Creator; but the Creator is infinite mercy, and to cultivate in ourselves habits of cruelty when He is infinite mercy is assuredly not fulfilling that duty. I think it to be certainly a sin and a crime to be cruel to animals, for the reasons I have given, not that it violates any rights the animals have, but because it is entirely opposed to the Divine injunction to fashion ourselves in the likeness of God. (Hear, hear).

Special Supplement to "The Zoophilist." London, Dec. 1st, 1893. National Anti-Vivsection Conference at Nottingham (specially reported). First day's proceedings.

I think vivisection, in practice, wholly abominable and detestable, and most dangerous to mankind.

I do not believe it has produced any good results, but, rather, many mischievous ones, especially that of diverting young medical men from legitimate study and dissection.

It is impossible that even a hundredth part of the atrocious cruelties which vivisectors (by their own account of themselves) spend their days in inflicting on helpless living creatures, can be practised without turning a man into something like a cruel Devil.

The developed taste for blood and cruelty must, in the end, find its full satisfaction in the vivisection of human beings, when they have the misfortune to come under the power of our future doctors. There is too much of it, I fear, going on already in our hospitals, and in practice among the poor.

✠ EDWARD, BISHOP OF NOTTINGHAM,

The Cathedral, Nottingham, Nov. 15*th*, 1895.

"*The Animals' Friend*," *January*, 1896.

At a demonstration held in St. James's Hall, London, in April, 1895, ARCHBISHOP BAGSHAWE said: Professor Slocum is reported to have said: "The aim of science is the advancement of human knowledge. If cats and guinea-pigs can be put to any better use than the advance of science, we do not know what it is. We do not know of any higher use that we can put a man to. Human life is nothing compared to a fact." That is the sort of state of mind that these men get into through their experimentation. Then he goes on: "After the furtherance of science, the saving of life is the noblest object we have in view." Hospitals, therefore, are for the advancement of science. We suppose when we subscribe to them that they are for the preservation of human life, and for the curing of disease. Then he says: "I think we, as medical men, should not attempt to conceal from the public the debt of gratitude we owe to the *corpora vilia*—to the wretched bodies of the poor—for such they are, and will be as long as the healing art exists and progresses." I will not read any further extracts; but these are sufficient to show that, in the opinion of these men, they might just as well experiment upon patients as they might upon cats and dogs and guinea-pigs. The *Zoophilist* of this month reproduces from the *Christian World* a paragraph from a German paper which says: "Numerous cases are cited where dangerous operations were performed simply to give the surgeons valuable experience. Many cases ended fatally, while in the others the victims were maimed for life; eighty cases are cited where children between the ages of eight and fifteen were inoculated with contagious diseases for experimental purposes. A similar outrage was committed upon a large number of women about to become mothers, whereby their innocent offspring were cursed by a terrible disease from the moment of their birth, and so on." (A voice: "Where—was that in England?") That was in Vienna. According to the *Zoophilist*, this report was verified afterwards, and these people excused themselves by saying that the same thing was practised in other places. I remember reading a case, not long ago, of some American who boasted that he had inoculated with yellow fever some half-dozen people, who had died in torments of it, and that man is not yet hanged. (Loud applause.) Then, I say, that besides leading to this, which I think is a terrible and grievous danger, vivisection is most mischievous in different ways.

Not only is it useless, but it is misleading. What are we to think of those doctors who, after vivisecting hundreds of dogs, find that they have drawn wrong conclusions, and have tried them probably on patients with infinite mischief? If it misleads it is worse than useless. If young medical men are to spend their lives in torturing animals because they hope that they may do something thereby to distinguish themselves, is it not turning them away altogether from their proper medical studies and *post-mortem* examinations, in which they can compare the symptoms of disease with what they find after death, and verify those symptoms and explain their meaning? Again, I think it is a serious evil that great distrust is created in the minds of many, certainly in my own, concerning hospitals, and those things going on there. We read of their managers considering the work of science as their first business. We read that they talk of their patients as "clinical material"—material for them to work upon. They are for enlarging the hospitals in order to get further available cases for their experiments. Without bringing, or wishing to bring, any accusation against so excellent a body of men as our doctors—and our friend Dr. Wall has just declared that he believes the great mass of them are innocent of these things—still it is a terrible thing that a suspicion of such things going on in our hospitals should exist, and if vivisection schools are attached to hospitals, it cannot be denied that there is good ground for such suspicion. (Cheers.) We have spoken of the great danger to humanity of its becoming the fashion to experiment upon people for practice, for money, for science, and for all manner of wrong motives, thereby incurring the guilt of being horribly cruel, and invading the just rights of men. But there is always the dreadful danger arising from the filthy poisons that medical men, or these experimentors at least, are cultivating, and making institutes to cultivate, here, there, and everywhere. Some of these serums are said to be "putrescent filth," they are all, I think, filled with all sorts of germs and poisons for spreading diseases. They are loathsome and abominable, and they are spread and cultivated, and hundreds of animals are inoculated with them; their carcases are turned out for the infection to be spread by all manner of creatures, such as mice, rats and flies. I say that to have laboratories to produce poisons and serums, and filthy remedies of this kind is a grievous danger to the human race. (Cheers.) Then, my resolution is, that these ought to be totally abolished by law. (Cheers.) You have heard—I think our own reason would tell us—that it is quite absurd to suppose that during two or three days of experiments on living animals, they can be kept under chloroform. It is difficult enough to do this for a short time in operations performed upon men, but to suppose that they do it for two or three days on end is a stretch of imagination which I cannot reach to. Moreover, it is acknowledged that 6,700 out of 8,000 odd of these experiments are done without even the pretence of anæsthetics. It is said that inoculation gives little pain, and it is perfectly true that it gives little pain at the moment. Are the agonies and the pains of poison and horrible diseases to be counted as nothing? (Applause.) Then as to the inspection. We have two medical men going twice a year to visit a laboratory, with notice given, and then they give in as their report the statement of the man himself. That is one of those farces which we are rather accustomed to—(laughter and applause)— the pretence of doing a thing to satisfy the public conscience, while we well know that we are not doing it. I will say no more, ladies and gentlemen, except that it is impossible to suppose that this system of giving licences to hundreds of persons to go on in secret doing these cruel things to animals, and with no possible adequate inspection of them, is protecting animals; it is increasing their danger, because now people cannot watch and observe, and report, and have the guilty punished for their doings. It is a shield under cover of which men can do as they like, and let their friends, and companions, and acquaintances come to their laboratories and do as they like.

It is impossible to suppose that the system of torture-chambers, increasing and multiplying over the country, can go on without these horrible abuses and dangers accompanying them. I say there is no possible remedy for the evils of vivisection but its total abolition. (Cheers.) Therefore, I propose to move that resolution.

Verbatim report of the speeches delivered at the great public demonstration at St. James's Hall, London, on Wednesday, April 26th. London: The London Anti-Vivisection Society, 1895.

THE INTERNATIONAL CONGRESS FOR ANIMAL PROTECTION.

Dr. LANDSTEINER: Ladies and gentlemen, if we were only all men of feeling, I should not begin my speech with polemics. But, alas! I must begin with a defence. It has been said here that the clergy do not interest themselves in the cause of kindness to animals. As the whole of the profession has been attacked, I must speak a few words of rejoinder, so that it may not be said that I was present and heard the accusation in silence, like a dumb dog. This reproach was made, and I cannot let it pass.

It has also been said that the Holy Scriptures contain nothing about the protection of animals, and that the spiritual authorities do not support the cause. That is unjust. Let us look round

this assembly . . . . . to say nothing
of the great Archbishop Manning, who was a
bright scientific light. Hosts of protectors of
animals fail to outweigh such a man as this, and
he was a Catholic Bishop. This alone should
prevent anyone speaking against the Catholic
Church. Even I, your humble servant, have
published a book, and it has been generally
acknowledged to be a valuable contribution towards teaching kindness to animals.

Mothers who send your sons to the University,
say to your children: "Will you, too, become
vivisectors? Will you act in opposition to the
hearts of your mothers? Rather than that, quit
the profession." This would have important
consequences. We have only courage to thunder
in Congress against what is painful to ourselves,
and elsewhere we have not the courage of our
opinions.

We shall, perhaps, resolve to do away with
vivisection, and I should support the measure
with all my heart. But we should then have done
but very little towards it. Much water will flow
down the Danube before the professors accept the
doctrine we preach. They attack the Jesuits
because they are supposed to say: "The end
justifies the means." But they themselves
exemplify this doctrine by practising the most
awful cruelties, to which the horrors of history are
nothing, as if they were mere children's sport.

General Report of the Twelfth International Congress for the Protection of Animals, at Buda-Pest, from 18th to 21st July, 1896. Published by the Society for the Protection of Animals, at Buda-Pest. Edited by the General Secretary of the Congress, Dr. Julius Syalkay.

THE MOST REV. P. J. RYAN,

Archbishop of Philadelphia.

DEAR MRS. WHITE,

I have always been touched by the beautiful expostulation of God addressed to the Prophet Jonah: "And shall I not spare Nineveh, that great city in which there are more than one hundred and twenty thousand persons that know not how to distinguish between their right hand and their left, and many beasts?"

The lower animals, so useful and often so affectionate and faithful, are dependent upon us, and it is cruel and sinful wantonly to torture them. If God has care for His birds of the air, and hears the voices of the young ravens crying out to Him for food, for they have on Him the claim of their creation, shall we who are, after all, the fellow-creatures of these beings, prove their only enemies? If the inspired Psalmist of Israel called on them to praise God, and the seraphic St. Francis of Assisi invited "our sisters the birds" to chant their vesper and matin hymns to Him who made them and vested them in glorious plumage, shall not we, inspired by similar sentiments, admire, cherish, and defend them? I congratulate you on being at the head of such an army of defence. It is a suitable and honorable post for a Christian woman.

P. J. RYAN.

The Fifteenth Report of the American Anti-vivisection Society. Philadelphia, 1898.

THE REV. DR. H. F. HENRY.

THE Fifteenth Annual Meeting of the American Anti-vivisection Society took place in Philadelphia in 1898, the President (Dr. Matthew Woods) in the chair.

The REV. H. F. HENRY.—Mr. President, Ladies, and Gentlemen : I can hardly claim the dignity of a lecturer on the subject of vivisection, nor can I even claim that I have written an address against vivisection. I really had intended coming here to-day merely to express my heartfelt sympathy with the movement. I believe I came through the kindness of the corresponding secretary, and to bid it God-speed in its splendid work. I feel honoured and highly gratified at the invitation to address you—an invitation of which, however, I do not mean to take advantage for any extended remarks. Although an enthusiastic supporter of the cause, I am a convert to it of such recent date that it would be scarcely within my ability, or my knowledge—as certainly it would hardly be within the limits of a proper modesty—to venture on a formal address before those who are so much better qualified by superior knowledge and ampler experience to treat interestingly the many-sided subject of vivisection. I desire rather to confine myself to offering the sincerest congratulations to this Society on the high ideal it cherishes and the splendid success it has attained. This success, indeed, falls far short of the ideal sought ; and, without any lessening of enthusiasm with respect to that ultimate desideratum, and without any sinking of the heart, our society is, doubtless, free to confess to a strong doubt whether it may hope to attain legislative enactment in our own generation prohibiting entirely the hideous practice against which it is warring.

Nevertheless, even should this never be attained, the societly may justly feel proud of the substantial results already obtained, and the promise these hold forth of still greater victories in the future. To my mind, the results gained by the activity of such societies as ours have been splendid, and have fully justified their existence and strenuous activity. While the tide of neo-barbarism, a pseudo-science of vivisection, was steadily invading the shores of our present-day refined civilisation, and threatening to engulf it in waves, not of water, but of blood, we have not watched the tide with the curious interest of King Canute of old, idly bidding the waves go "thus far and no farther"; rather have we imitated the better industry of the men of Holland, and have been building strong dykes to restrain its onward progress. We may not have conquered the sea; but, at least, we have been actively engaged in saving the land.

That hideous cruelty has not wholly triumphed; that it has assumed the character of apology rather than of insolent confidence; that its deeds of darkness have been displayed to the world in all their deformity, and in the pitiless glare of God's sunlight; that the public conscience is being stirred at last; that the highest professions have hastened to enrol their greatest names in this movement, names of eminent Churchmen, statesmen, physicians, lawyers; that a benign interest in the dumb creatures of our Heavenly Father, taking the form of a generous propagandism of mercy in their behalf, has ceased to be characterised as a "fad," and has assumed the dignity of a fact—all these great achievements must have remained but a pathetic dream of a few tender-hearted men and women were it not for the militant organisation represented by such societies as ours.

But these excesses, while they have not taken away from the veneration due to science, have taught the world the necessity of a discrimination between it and its professors. Like the man in the Gospel, "Whereas we were blind, we now see." A person who sits down to reflect would, doubtless, make a discrimination *a priori*. The world at large, however, does not take the time to reflect, and is, therefore, apt to esteem as an unquestioned fact the merest surmises of the scientist. When these surmises appear in the guise of a benefit to suffering humanity; when we are assured that a little suffering on the part of a brute animal will lead to an immunity from suffering on the part of the human animal, and that this immunity, once obtained at such a small price, will be of enduring value—I say it is not to be wondered at that the world simply applauds without investigating, and believes without proving. The literature distributed by this society is calculated thoroughly to remove this delusion from the mind of the public, and to establish a most desirable distinction between the merest guess-work and a rational inference, between a wanton infliction of suffering, a blundering theory in blood-shedding, and a well-ordered, sensible procedure, looking to the amelioration of the lot of humanity. These truths will appeal to many, who, perhaps, would remain unaffected by any argument based on the immorality of the practice of vivisection.

There are, however, many to whom such a plea will appeal most powerfully, and it is to me personally, as an humble representative of the Church of the Ages, a source of high gratification to find Cardinal Manning basing a splendid reasoning on this ground, appealing, not to sentiment, but to rigorous logic, and withal testifying, by the impassioned eloquence of his language, to a personal conviction, deeply rooted in the finest soil of his heart.

I need not rehearse before this society the long and strenuous labours of this eminent dignitary, nor the trumpet-like utterances of our own American Cardinal on the same subject of vivisection. The point I desire to make is that if the names of such lights in medicine as Sir W. Ferguson, Sir Charles Bell, and Lawson-Tait, and the names of the eminent physicians in our land who have given their suffrages to the cause—if these names, carrying with them such great weight of authority in their several spheres, be placed before the people in such a way that "they who run may read," then must the great obstacle of ignorance be removed. This work the society is doing. I had proposed speaking of the other two obstacles encountered by the movement—namely, sloth and selfishness—and how well the work of this society tends to overcome them. But I fear I am running into a set address, a thing which your courtesy might indeed tolerate, but which my own limitations forbid. But as for the obstacle of indifference, that, I say, the society is removing constantly. I suppose you must be very patient in that line, because deep-seated evils require a long-continued treatment; and again, when we war against the world-wide wilfulness, selfishness, and ignorance which are the main-stays of vivisection, we must expect to make slow progress, and in this line I wish again to bid it God-speed.

The Fifteenth Annual Report of the American Anti-vivisection Society for the total abolition of all vivisectional experiments on animals, and other experiments of a painful nature.

FATHER LESCHER, O P.

Whatever meaning may be given to the word *Rights*, I intend to show that, in animals there is a something—call it right or call it claim—which is an intrinsic bar to cruelty, and renders that cruelty a sin.

In other words, there is a real objective counterpart to the acknowledged sin of cruelty to animals, and that it is to be found in the animal's nature. Cardinal Zigliara says: *Peccatum est crudelitas etiam in bestiis*, because thereby the cruel person *ponit actionem dissonam a fine et ordine Creatoris*. Words could not more clearly point to an objective law. He denies to animals *jura*, and by these he evidently understands rights in their high human sense only.

It is strange, indeed, to hear it put forward as an axiom that animals have no rights. As an academic proposition it might pass, but it would then assuredly never merit discussion for it is in that sense a truism. But when put forward in order to justify vivisection, we begin to see that in it there is a grim something which calls for strong opposition. For it is used as a cover to the grossest cruelties and the most frightful abuses. It is meant in earnest to justify animals being used as the toys of man's torturing and tearing instruments, as the objects of his vicious caprice to assert a dominion over them as absolute and as despotic as over the trees and shrubs of the earth. Its most vehement assertors cannot defend it. For, if animals have no rights, it follows that there is no such thing as cruelty to animals, or that cruelty to animals is not wrong. They do not, they dare not, assert that consequence. Of what use, then, is the proposition, except to fortify a dangerous practice, and to put a convenient sophistry into the vivisector's hand?

That an animal has a distinct place in creation, that it has a relation to man above a plant is distinctly laid down by St. Thomas. He treats of the dominion of man over other creatures, and he says that his dominion over plants and other lower things is unlimited. Man uses them, *absque impedimento*. Cajetan, the first of Thomist commentators, says that man over these *habet dominium despoticum*. But his dominion over animals is limited. The limit is their own living

KINDNESS TO ANIMALS.

and sensitive nature, which reason tells us is higher and better than inanimate natures, subject to less of law and more entitled to freedom.

It is difficult to believe that the *open sesame* of science is only to be found in the cries of the animal creation at the expense of man's demoralization. There are some also, we must not forget, who deny that these facts are of any use, or have caused any good. Authorities of undoubted worth have declared this, which shows that the boasting of vivisectors proves a great deal too much.

Further, granting the use, it must be subject to the general good, and that good is paramount in the general morality. The people recognise that the treatment of animals is a moral question. The Acts against cruelty are a sufficient proof that the country is agreed to place absolutely the reasonable and humane treatment of animals above their mere utility. That animals are meant, in the Providential order of things, to educate both the thought and affection of man, is proved by the fact that they have that influence. The wrong treatment of them must produce a distorted character, as experience shows. No one will deny that great and habitual cruelty in a child towards animals is rightly looked on everywhere as a very bad augury, and is the proof of a depraved disposition.

To hear the speech of vivisectionists we might almost regard this as an antiquated idea. The common sense of mankind will, however, assert itself, and will assuredly continue to regard kindness to animals as an index to private character, and the laws which injure it as harmful to the national character itself.

As to the theological aspect of vivisection, I have said enough to show that the principles of a satisfactory solution are contained in Catholic theology. The kernel of the matter is in man's dominion over creatures. St. Thomas treats of that distinctly. The corresponding term is in the animal's nature. Here the question has not yet been treated adequately, but enough is said to point in the same direction, and to show that the subjective law has an objective counterpart.

"*The Practice of Vivisection,*" *by Wilfrid Lescher, O.P. Stroud: J. Elliot, Stroudwater Printing Office.* 1894.

A letter by FATHER LESCHER, O.P., *published in* "*The Catholic Times and Catholic Opinion*," *of Friday, November* 11*th*, 1898.

SIR,—It does not seem extravagant to say that animals have got rights. It is true that they have not human rights; but as there is in them a nature demanding a treatment quite above that accorded to wood or iron, plants and shrubs (as St. Thomas says), so it is reasonable to claim for them rights—animal rights. There is no theological or philosophical consensus against this proposition, which we should hold all the more firmly as we see the opposite favoured by the advocates and defenders of vivisection. Animals are not mere things, nor would any civilized law allow them to be treated as such.

Yours, &c.,
WILFRID LESCHER, O.P.

November 7th, 1898.

CARDINAL GIBBONS.

The old law commanded: "Thou shalt not muzzle the ox when he treadeth out the corn." Certainly the law of Christ is not less benevolent to the creatures that minister to the comfort and needs of man.

    Faithfully yours in Christ,
      ✠ J. CARDINAL GIBBONS.

H. E. Cardinal Gibbons, Archbishop of Baltimore, on Humanity towards Animals in the Old and the New Law. " The Animals' Friend," January, 1896.

THE RIGHT REV. ABBOT GASQUET, O.S.B.

Article 1.—How our fathers were taught in Catholic days.

Some few years ago, I attempted in the pages of this Review, to show that the instruction given by the English priests in pre-Reformation times was by no means so hopelessly inadequate as it suited the sectarian purposes of some writers to represent. In fact, an extended and careful examination of original and much-neglected sources had compelled me to come to a very different conclusion.

The volume I propose to submit to the test of examination is one that is said to have been very popular in the fifteenth century. It is called *Dives et Pauper*—the rich and the poor man—and its purpose is thus declared in the colophon at the end of one copy: "Here endeth a compendious treatise or dialogue of Dives and Pauper: that is to say, the rich and the poor, fructuously treating upon the Ten Commandments." The fact that it was considered a volume of sufficient interest and importance to warrant its publication by the first English printers among the earliest fruits of the newly-discovered art of printing, will be sufficient to attest its popularity, and the value attached to it by the ecclesiastical authorities.

After carefully reading the volume, and noting any illustrations of the time and of the circumstances of the English people when the author was writing, I am strongly of opinion that the book was composed somewhere in the first decade of the fifteenth century.

The passages quoted will be given as in the original, but, for the convenience of the reader, in a modern spelling.

It is somewhat curious at a time when, as we have been led to suppose, cruelty, especially to animals, was little considered, to find our author speaking strongly against the wanton and unnecessary killing of God's creatures.

"When God bade man to eat flesh" (he says) " He forbade him to slay beasts in any cruel way, or, out of any liking for shrewness. Therefore, He said : 'Eat ye no flesh with blood' (Genesis ix.), that is to say, with cruelty, 'for I shall seek the blood of your souls at the hands of all beasts.' That is to say : I shall take vengeance for all the beasts that are slain only out of cruelty of soul and a liking for shrewness. For God that made all, hath care of it all, and he will take vengeance upon all that misuse His creatures. Therefore, Solomon saith : ' That He will arm creatures in vengeance on their enemies' (Sap. v.), and so men should have thought for birds and beasts, and not harm them without cause, in taking regard that they are God's creatures. Therefore. they that, out of cruelty and vanity, behead beasts, and torment beasts or fowl more than is proper for man's living, they sin in case full grievously."

The Right Rev. Abbot Gasquet, Councillor of the Pontifical Commission of the Churches of the East, on the Teaching of Kindness to Animals by the Churches in the Middle Ages. " The Dublin Review," April, 1897.

THE "FAMILY CATECHISM."

We have precepts as to the treatment of animals. The fifth commandment forbids men to hunt and worry animals unnecessarily, and rather commands them, on the contrary, to be merciful. God has made man lord over all the earth, and all animals are given into his hands. He may make use of them, and drive away those which are dangerous, but he must take care of those which serve him; and, if he must kill animals, he must do so as painlessly as possible. Especial care and attention must be shown to tame animals, as they cannot help themselves, nor complain, but are entirely at man's mercy. What would man do without animals?

Is it, then, not shameful when a man, with unfeeling brutality, intentionally causes pain to an animal, or causes it injury by his thoughtlessness and neglect? Like man, an animal has five senses, and can feel pain. Even for his own sake, man should be indulgent to domestic animals. The Holy Scriptures, however, expressly command it. "The righteous man takes care of his beast, but the heart of the godless is cruel." (Proverbs xii. 10.) The following rules should be especially observed:—When an animal is to be killed, it should be done so that death may be hastened as much as possible, and so that all unnecessary pain may be avoided. Of what horrors do not men make themselves guilty? We have only to think of the gagged calves, sheep, and pigs; of the ill-treated cart-horses, the baited bulls, and the fish boiled alive.

Whoever feels no pity when he sees a calf tied up in a cart in the heat of summer, exposed to be stung by flies—when he sees the animal quite helpless, with its tongue hanging out, with its head banged about in the cart, then taken out and thrown on the ground, and left to lie there day and night—whoever sees that and similar sights, and feels no pity, and no wish to prevent such cruelty, does not deserve the name of a man, and is no child of the Heavenly Father, of whom it is said: "He gives the cattle their food, and feeds the young ravens that call upon Him." (Ps. cxlvi. 9.) "Are not two sparrows sold for a farthing? And not one of them is forgotten before God." (Luke xii. 6.)

EXAMPLES.

How much care the Lord Himself shows towards creatures devoid of reason we see very clearly in the history of Jonah. For when this disobedient prophet murmured because Nineveh was not destroyed, the Lord said to Him: "And should I not spare Nineveh, that great city, wherein are more than a hundred and twenty thousand persons who cannot discern between their right hand and their left, *and also many animals?"* (Jonah iv. 11.)

Moses gave the Israelites strict laws, intended to promote forbearance to animals: "Thou shalt not see thy brother's ox or his sheep go astray, and pass them by; thou shalt, in any case, bring them again unto thy brother." (Deut. xxii. 1.) "Thou shalt not see thy brother's ass or his ox fall down by the way: thou shalt not contemn to help him in lifting them up again." (Deut. xxii. 4.) And the same law is to be observed in the case of an enemy's ox or ass. "Thou shalt not plough with an ox and an ass together." (Deut. xxii. 10.)

Even temporal blessings are promised to him who is indulgent to animals. For Moses said: "If thou find, as thou walkest by the way, a bird's nest in a tree, or on the ground, and the dam sitting upon the young or upon the eggs, thou shalt not take her with her young: but thou shalt let her go and keep the young: that it may be well with thee, and thou mayest live long." (Deut. xxii. 67.)

It was the custom among the Israelites to tread out the corn with oxen. There were avaricious people who muzzled the oxen while at work, to prevent their eating any of it. Therefore, it was commanded: "Thou shalt not muzzle the mouth of the ox which threshes out the fruits of the threshing floor." (Deut. xxv. 4.)

In the third commandment it is also expressly ordered that even an animal was not to work on the Sabbath. "Six days shalt thou work, and the seventh day shalt thou rest, that thine ox and thine ass may rest." (Ex. xxiii. 12.) Indeed, to cherish tender mercy in the Israelites, it was commanded: "Thou shalt not seethe a kid in his mother's milk." (Exodus xxiii. 19.)

By the Rev. Dr. Rolfus, with letters of approbation from the Bishops of Mayence, Limburg, Linz, Basle, Lugano, and St. Gall.

THE RIGHT REV. PRELATE LANDSTEINER.

The *Tales by the Rector of Kirchthal* show what man may become by the good or bad treatment of animals. The friend of animals, the brave Michael, is contrasted with the wicked persecutor of animals, and otherwise worthless Kilian. While the latter sinks by degrees till he perishes as a criminal, Michael rises and becomes a rich and respected landowner. The whole reminds one of Hogarth's characteristic representation of the career of the industrious and the idle apprentice, and is also a kind of "Good Fridolin and wicked Dietrich," from the standpoint of protection of animals.

DR. LANDSTEINER'S PREFACE TO THE SECOND EDITION.

I describe this edition of the tales of the priest of Kirchthal as the second edition, although the book in its original form went through many editions. It is, however, the second edition of my arrangement of the work. This time the Viennese Protection of Animals Society has, at my suggestion, especially taken up the beautiful little work, and brought out at its own expense an illustrated edition of it. By this means the Society is enabled to make the book known in its own circles. The beautiful ornamentation of the book makes it suitable for a birthday present.

"*Tales by the Rector of Kirchthal,*" *by Wilhelm Podlaha. New edition. With a life-sketch of the author, by Charles Landsteiner.* (*Vienna: Published by the Viennese Society for the Protection of Animals in* 1896. *William Podlaha's* "*Life and Work.*")

CARDINAL RAMPOLLA.

Answer to a letter addressed by the Council of the Paris Society for the Protection of Animals to Leo XIII.

"Most Illustrious Sir,

"The expressions of gratitude and devotion contained in a letter of the 17th February, which was addressed to our Holy Father by your illustrious self, and which was also sent in the name of the administrative Council of the Society over which you preside, were at once accepted by his paternal heart, especially because of the highly humanitarian and Christian aims of your Society.

"For these reasons, he deigns to express to you, through me, his due thanks. Offering you my deep esteem, I remain, etc.,

"CARDINAL RAMPOLLA.

" Rome, *February* 24th, 1894.
" To the most illustrious Alberto Uhlrich."

Report of the Society for the Protection of Animals, in Paris, March, 1894.

CARDINAL DONNET.

SPEAKING at an Agricultural Meeting in France in 1866, CARDINAL DONNET said: Gentlemen,—Not long ago I called upon the meeting at Bazas to admire a bee-hive. To-day I shall speak to you on a subject for which I cannot fail to have your sympathy. I wish to make you kind and compassionate.

I shall not speak to you of charitable devotion to your brethren. I shall not talk to you of the wonders of public and private charity. But if, as I like to bear witness, you are just and good to each other, why should you not also be just, good, and compassionate to the animals which help you to make your land productive, and to distribute its fruits? Our power over the creatures which surround us comes from God Himself. It has pleased Him who created the world to put us over them, and to make animals obey us. "Let us make man, and set him over all things that live." But to this authority God has annexed duties from which we are not allowed to withdraw. By placing animals under us He has commanded us to be full of pity for them. We are not to turn against them those advantages which Providence has given us in order that we may rule them wisely.

The protection due to animals is partly embodied in a recent enactment with which the public has connected the name of an illustrious general, a man of our own district. But it would be of little use to make a law if the sense of duty were not engraven on our people's hearts, and if the support given to it by our writers had not already found an echo in all ranks of society. This law does not seem to have, so far, been enough applied, nor has it produced the results which might have been expected from it when I first spoke to you about it all too briefly. In a circular dated August 20, 1859, the Minister of the Interior again calls the attention of the local authorities to the necessity of taking efficient measures to ensure its operation. For my part, I applaud every sort of effort of the monthly circulars issued on behalf of animals. This energetic start gives a hope that, from theory, the ideas of compassion may pass into conduct, which is more powerful than laws.

The Church, by the voice of her Sovereign

Pontiffs, has placed herself at the head of the movement. It is for her to take the lead whenever she can make herself heard. Human passions are revealed in the disastrous excesses which are found everywhere in nature; and religion has simply to combat them wherever they show themselves. It is in this sense that it has been said that the power of the Redemption has descended on all creatures, and that its merciful Author would restore the whole world. "To restore all things in Christ!" Who does not recognise the influence of cupidity and anger even upon animals which are under the sway of man? One cannot, then, blame the priest who speaks on behalf of them, and who, in protecting them, protects their masters also against that which brings degradation.

The government of animals imposes two duties on man : that of taking care of them in making use of them, and that of sparing them all useless suffering. Here there is no question of showing irrational animals excessive attentions in the way of affection, and a liberality of gifts denied to our fellow creatures. But, if we condemn irresponsible emotions and excess of sentiment as ridiculous as it is unprofitable, we still more strongly condemn insensibility, and the sordid selfishness which disregards the warning of St. Paul that, where the ox draws the furrow, it is right to prepare straw for the litter and hay for the manger, as it is wrong to enfeeble the beast by stinting his fodder. "Thou shalt not muzzle the mouth of the ox that treadeth out the corn."

Such would be the wrong done by a landowner who aimed at an absurd economy in feeding his flocks or his teams, speculating also on the profits of sales by fattening his stock in ways hurtful to the health of his animals, or who abandoned the care of his farms to paid servants. Those, again, would be wicked who, through negligence, allowed the grain or the grass to deteriorate, speculating in their turn in fraudulent robbery of poor creatures powerless to report to their masters the disloyal and cruel proceedings of their salaried tyrants, who expose them without pity to the inclemency of the seasons, leave them night after night on unwholesome straw, and refuse to take those easy precautions which prevent illness, preserve from injuries, and guarantee both strength and health.

One link overlaps another, gentlemen, in the chain of evil; and if we describe in commonest detail these pictures of human carelessness, it is to remind men that they are neglectful of animals only because they allow their consciences to rust in shameful apathy.

The Holy Spirit bids the idle to consider the ant, and be ashamed of their indolence. We would also bid the greedy landowners, the unfaithful farmers, to consider their flocks and herds, and see the results of their negligence, and the ills occasioned by their love of gambling, dissipation, and irregular life.

The second duty imposed on man towards animals is summed up in that word of such wide meaning—*humanity*.

We are, gentlemen, far removed from that too short period when man, created in innocence and submission to his Creator, saw all the animals come to him, and bear the yoke of his authority without fear. Now, every thing that lives and breathes fears his shadow even, and flees at his

KINDNESS TO ANIMALS. 181

approach. This terror is, without doubt, one of the punishments incurred by the first sin, which broke man's union with God.

But is not this terror our work also? From the beginning, the only exceptions to this rule are about a dozen different domestic animals. Even the majority of them would have a right to accuse us of barbarism if they could hand down from generation to generation the particulars of the evils which they have had to endure, sometimes by over-work and sometimes through ill-treatment.

Animals have only a certain amount of strength, and their activities are finite. Age and infirmity set them limits, which vary with climate and dispositions. As long as we respect these limits, strength increases, life expands, and their bodies increase in value, because they can do more work. But, if you overstep these limits, you tempt the Creator, and you prevent the plans of His Providence. Hence, the Divine Wisdom reveals this maxim: " God hath arranged everything in number, measure, and weight."

Every animal should have the distance measured which he has to go; the burden he has to bear should not exceed a certain weight; he is only fit to work a certain number of hours in the day and of days in the week. It is the universal law of being, the Divine dispensation! It can never be transgressed with impunity. The fields would be exhausted if they were not renewed by rest. To scatter seed over them indiscriminately would exhaust their fertility; to move the soil beyond measure would cause the nourishing juices to evaporate. Agriculture prospers as much by the law of rest as by the law of work. Why should not the animal races be subject to the same conditions of life or death, and increase or decrease in strength, according as man respects or violates with regard to them the maxim already quoted: *Omnia mensura, numero et pondere disposuit Dominus*?

Ah, without occupying himself with agricultural problems, or the methods of feeding, but by the sole fact of the command he exercises over himself, and the regular habits he has formed, the religious man becomes gentle, moderate, and humane in the tribute of work he exacts from his animals. He follows up their aptitudes. They are, moreover, the working part of his estate; they are his productive capital in the sweat of suffering; he sees in them the companions of his labours, and he takes good care not to cut them off from his affection and compassion. Moreover, wherever evangelical piety flourishes, it spreads orderliness over the country districts. We get a glimpse of it in the order and silence of the sheep, heifers, and bullocks, whether grazing on the hills, or drinking at the stream, or returning to the sheds, or drawing carts and carriages. Everything is managed with prudence, and watched over with a kind of affection. It is only necessary to go over the farms of the Trappists, or the Carthusians, or those of the orphans of St. Louis de Rioux, or of Couberac, or the properties cultivated by some of the patriarchal families which have kept up their religious habits, in order to see the fatherly oversight of the work, and the happy results of such oversight.

One cannot too often tell the farm servants, drivers, and carters, that in overloading, in making

KINDNESS TO ANIMALS.

over-long journeys, in inflicting, according to their caprice, cruel blows on their oxen or horses, they commit a barbarism for which they will pay dearly.

And now, gentlemen, on behalf of that compassion for animals which I would fain have you to feel, let me relate to you a scene which will make amends for the brutality which you so often witness. I wish to show you two sportsmen in the pose of a Sister of Charity, kneeling, not before a soldier wounded at Solferino, but before a thrush which has fallen wounded by the shots of one of them. The most experienced of the two wished to apply a dressing to the wounded thigh, and he was already preparing it. The other one pleaded for a system which he had already used with success in treating fractures in birds. No one will be angry with me for dwelling on these small details. The practical and salutary lessons we can learn from them are evident to everybody.

Look at these two impromptu doctors carefully placing their invalid in a basket filled with thick moss. A cloth is placed over the top to make it dark, and prevent the poor bird from dashing against it head foremost. It allowed all these things to be done. By insensible degrees it came to look without trembling on those who, instead of its murderers, had become its saviours. Now this suffering thrush was to have its record among the annals of a castle enriched with many recollections, one which had received guests famous in quite other ways than this. One day, as the family were standing round the convalescent bird, one of them opened an old book which occupied a place of honour in the rich library, because it had been written by a former owner of the place, and they heard the following maxims beautifully read by an excellent reader:

"I find that our greatest vices take their rise from bad habits of our earliest infancy, and that our chief government is in the hands of our nurses. It is an amusement to mothers to see a child twist the neck of a fowl, or beat a dog or a cat till it is injured. These are, however, the seeds and roots of cruelty. There they germinate and grow quite gaily."

This first lord of the castle, moralist and animal protector, was a former Mayor of Bordeaux: he was Montaigne.

"Report of the Society for the Protection of Animals." October, 1866. *Paris. Extract from Cardinal Donnet's Speech at the Agricultural Meeting of the District of Blaye, Sant-Savin, September 3rd*, 1866.

M. L'ABBÉ DE RAEMY.

SPEAKING at Geneva in 1900, he said: One word more on vivisection. The greatest doctors and the most learned professors of anatomy have loudly denounced the uselessness, even more the abuse and the dangers, of the barbarous experiments resorted to in some medical amphitheatres on living animals without anæthestics. Moreover, we deny any such practioner the right of calling himself a protector of animals. Here is the protest which, as President of this Union, I have addressed to the Thirteenth International Congress, which held meetings at Paris from the 16th to the 20th of June:

"I join my protest to that of the *Zoophilist* Society of Magdeburg against the prejudice which would exclude the anti-vivisectionists from the deliberations of the Congress for the Protection of Animals. In my opinion, vivisection is one of the least acceptable forms of scientific barbarism.

"Far from being necessary or useful to the progress of medical science, it hardens the hearts of medical students, and tempts them to renew on human subjects the experiments they have already seen made upon animals.

"We also take the opportunity, without any feeling of hostility towards Jews, to protest against their method of killing cattle. This method is superannuated, and is not in accord with either the letter or the spirit of the law of Moses, and it ought to be forbidden in all civilised countries.

"ABBÉ CH. DE RAEMY,

"President of the Romande Union."

If we are obliged to put animals to death, let us at least do it with kindness, and spare them the horrors of a death struggle. Therefore, let us join with Monsignor Besson in denouncing bullfights, those cruel sports which, after disgracing

Spain, have crossed the Pyrenees, and become rooted in France, and have even reached the gates of Paris.

Opening Speech of the President, Abbé Charles de Raemy, at the General Assembly at Geneva, October 2nd, 1900.

CARDINAL VAUGHAN,

Archbishop of Westminster.

AN esteem for knowledge and instruction, a strong temperance movement against animal excesses, provision for the sick and helpless, a thoughtful care even for dumb animals, faithful servants of man, all these things have sprung up during this reign, and are clearly matter for thanksgiving to Him who, in a true sense, is the inspirer and the finisher of all good works.

"*The Queen's Jubilee.*" *Pastoral by Cardinal Vaughan : The Tablet, London, June* 19, 1897.

DOM HUNTER BLAIR, O.S.B., BART.

THE CHAIRMAN, at a meeting of friends of animals, held at Oxford, said: Before saying a few words which, as Chairman, it was his privilege to do by way of striking the key-note of this meeting, he wished to read them a letter, because it expressed what they would like to hear, and what he could not tell them himself, about a friend to Anti-vivisection whom they had lately lost. The other day he had a talk with Sir David Hunter Blair, who had come to settle amongst them as the head of Blair's Hall. He was glad to welcome him as a strong and convinced Anti-vivisectionist, and especially because the Roman Church had been maligned owing to some of its members having spoken of animals as having no rights. Sir David Hunter Blair had the courage of his opinions. They were talking the other day, and he expressed his regret that an engagement of longer standing had prevented his attending this meeting. He wished him, however, to bring before the meeting some reference to Lord Bute, who was not only a convinced Anti-vivisectionist, but one who had done yeoman service to the cause. (Applause.) He ventured to say to him that he knew more about the late Lord Bute than he (the chairman) did, and suggested that he should write a letter which might be read. The letter was as follows:

My Dear Master,

Lord Bute often spoke to me with dislike and horror of the practice of vivisection, and had a strong opinion as to the anomalousness and inadequacy of the laws by which the practice is supposed to be regulated and restricted in this country. He was Vice-President of the National Antivivisection Society for many years, and, in the days when his health allowed him, often attended the committee meetings. I believe he was present at the very first general meeting of the society. He gave considerable sums, both directly and indirectly, in furtherance of the aims of the society, and he subscribed £100 to the testimonial to Miss Cobbe when she retired from the hon. secretaryship. When the Cardiff Infirmary was made over to University College, Lord Bute (who was a trustee) refused to sign the deed of transference except on the condition that the College should undertake that vivisection should never be practised within the walls of the infirmary.

You will, I am sure, agree with me that these facts might suitably be communicated to the meeting at which you preside on the 20th inst. Lord Bute's feelings on this matter were not of recent growth: they dated from his undergraduate days at Christ Church in 1886 and 1887, at which period he often conversed on the subject with his, and our, lamented friend, Miss Felicia

Shene, and expressed his deep dislike to the practices which our Society has since been founded to oppose.

Pray let me add to this note the expression of my own sincere regret that an engagement of long standing prevents my having the pleasure of assisting at a meeting with whose objects I am so cordially in sympathy.

Yours very truly,

DAVID HUNTER BLAIR, O.S.B.

" *The Zoophilist and Animals' Defender.*" *London, December 1st,* 1900.

J. STAPF.

GOD has endued even animals with a sense of the joy of life, according to their measure. Far be it, then, from us to injure this sense of theirs in any way, or to inflict pain and suffering on them out of mere cruelty of heart. But such a habit of treating animals badly always pre-supproses a low ferocity of mind. For anyone at all humane is repelled by such delight in torment, and is touched with pity when he sees poor animals in great pain, whether by accident or from some just cause. In short, feelings of humanity become more and more blunted by such cruelty to animals. Whoever is accustomed to be heartless towards brute beasts will soon be cruel to men and devoid of all brotherly pity. Experience abundantly proves this. The feeling of kindness to animals breathes through the pages of the Old Testament, and is evident from many passages, *e.g.*, Exodus xxiii. 5 ; Deut. xxv. 4 ; Prov. xii. 10 ; Eccli. vii. 24.

Theol. Mor. in comp. redac. ab Ambr. Jos. Stapf, Tom. II. ; ed. quarta ; Œneponte, 1838.

P. SCAVINI.

DOMINION OVER ANIMALS.—Two things are to be guarded against in the treatment of animals: doting fondness and inhuman cruelty. The first is unworthy of a rational being. Those are certainly to be blamed who are so attached to pets as to prize them above their fellow men. Nevertheless, reason abhors all wanton cruelty towards animals, for this is repugnant to the Divine plans. For God has endued animals with a sense of the joy of life according to their measure.

Theol. Mor. Universa ad mentem S. Alphonsi de Lig. auct. P. Scavini ; Ed. XIV. ; Liber II. ; Mediolani, 1890.

NOTES.

The Archbishop of Madras wrote to the *Catholic Watchman* (Madras) the following letter, dated February 13th, 1905:—

DEAR SIR,—I have been requested by the Executive Committee of the Society for the Prevention of Cruelty to Animals to fix a Sunday to be called the Animal Sunday, for sermons in promoting the objects of the Society. I have much pleasure in bringing this matter to the notice of the Catholic Priests in this Archdiocese, and trust that as far as possible they will accede to the wishes of the Committee, and earnestly recommend to their respective flocks the claims the dumb animals have on their sympathetic support.

Believe me, yours very truly,
J. COLGAN, Archbishop of Madras.

The eagerness of St. Francis to make his *protégés* praise their Creator is commemorated by the fifth antiphon of the praises sung by his Order on his birthday:

> *Laudans laudare monuit,*
> *Laus illi semper adfuit*
> *Laus inquam, Salvatoris:*
> *Invitat aves, bestias, et creaturas alias*
> *Ad laudem Conditoris.*

And his relations with birds are again recalled in the antiphon of the Magnificat of the second Vespers:

> *Dat aurem suis avium prædicans silvestrium verbis intendentem.*

The birds, which play such a beautiful part in many of these stories, had the same gracious relations with other ascetics. We remember the raven which every day carried half a loaf to St. Paul the Hermit, and which did not fail to furnish a whole one on the occasion of St. Antony's visit. Another raven, on the contrary, came to Subiaco, and begged of St. Boniface a part of each of his meals. To these incidents, attested, the one by St. Jerome and the other by St. Gregory the Great, let us add what is said of St. Guthlac, an English hermit who died at the beginning of

the eighth century. The swallows came and twittered round
him, and perched on his shoulders and knees and on his head
or breast; and he, on his side, with his own hands built them
nests in little baskets with rushes and pieces of straw, which
he placed under the thatch of his cell, where each year the
dear little guests came to seek their accustomed homes.
"Oh, my father," said an astonished visitor, "how have you
been able to inspire such confidence in these daughters of
solitude?" "Do you not know," replied the hermit, "that he
who unites himself to God in purity of heart in his turn sees
His creatures unite themselves to him? The birds of heaven,
like the angels, frequent those who do not frequent the society
of mankind." We already know that in the Grande Chartreuse
he tamed both birds and squirrels by his gentleness. At
Witham he had kept the same ascendency, and for three
years he could be seen with a brownish bird, a kind of wild
goose, which came with confidence to the good Prior's cell,
and ate from his hand the crumbs he had collected for it. It only
left the man of God when it was sitting on its eggs, and then re-
appeared followed by its little ones. Its remembrance, however, has remained much less vivid than that of the swan, the
dealings of which with our holy Bishop we have to recount.
One of the esteemed authors of the time, Gerald of Cambria,
who passed several years at Lincoln under the episcopate of
St. Hugh, was an ocular witness ot these facts, and described
them during the life of our Saint. As an observer, he examined
the swan attentively, and the description he has left of it
corresponds almost entirely to that given by naturalists of the
wild swan, of which the beak, the head, und the neck are
shaded with yellow.—*Life of St. Hugh, Monk of the Chartreuse,
Bishop of Lincoln* (1140-1200). *By a Monk of the Grande Chartreuse.* 1900. The kindness of St. Hugh of Lincoln to
animals was also celebrated shortly after his death in a life
of him that has come down to us in hexameters. The great
Prelate, so kind to the small, was able to hold his own in
defending the oppressed and the rights of the Church against
Sovereigns as intractable as the Kings of England, Henry II.,
Richard I., and John. He is one of the Patrons of the Car-
thusian Order, in whose garb he is to be seen in a picture of
Ludovic of Parma, now in the National Gallery in London.
The painter of the "Apparition of the Child Jesus to St. Hugh,"
in the Chartreuse of Paris, has not omitted to place the faithful
and well-beloved swan in the picture.

Paul II. was one of the most pious and virtuous persons of
his age, and a great Pontiff. It is much to be regretted that
the memory of so illustrious a soul should have suffered
through the malignity of Platina, his most-read historian up to

ST. ANTHONY THE HERMIT AND HIS HOG.
(*Nicolo Pisano.*) See p. 193.

this time, who wished to revenge himself on the Pontiff for a well-merited digrace.

The life in Portuguese of the Venerable Joseph of Anchieta by Father Vasconcellos, of the Company of Jesus (Lisbon, 1672), is ornamented by a beautiful plate as frontispiece, which represents the "Miracle-worker of the New World" surrounded by animals of all kinds to which in some way or other he had shown kindness. The following account of his doings with wild animals is by M. Henri Bourgeois, in *Saints and Animals*, a publication of the Society of St. Augustine, with the official appreciation of the Bishop of Luçon and the imprimatur of the Archbishop of Cambray, also a medal from the Society for the Protection of Animals in Paris (Descleé de Brouwer and Co). This noble servant of God was born in 1534 in one of the Canary Islands, and at the age of seventeen he entered the Company of Jesus. Sent as a missionary to Brazil for forty-four years, he preached the Gospel among the idolatrous populations of the New World, and the power which he obtained over wild animals in the course of his mission obtained for him from biographers the name of the Second Adam. The birds were particularly his friends; he had them constantly about him. In whatever house he was entertained they flew to greet him at the window, and would allow themselves to be caught and caressed by him; they would not go until he had given them his blessing. When he was travelling, whether across forests or by rivers, or even by sea, the dear little things would bear him company, and perch on his shoulders and even on his breviary; and more than once this touching familiarity led to the conversion of a number of savages, who saw the work of God in this marvellous power over creatures. So true is it that God knows how to make the smallest means, even the kindness of the Saints towards animals, serve His ends. One day, when the holy missionary had embarked on the sea for a distant mission, a number of parrots, lost and fatigued, came to settle on the vessel. The sailors and passengers rushed on the poor birds, who would have had a bad time of it had not Father Anchieta taken them under his protection, and prevented their being hurt. The grateful parrots immediately flocked to perch on his shoulders, and he did not cease to caress them until the end of the voyage. When the vessel came to the shore, the good father petted them for the last time (they did not appear to like leaving him), and then dismissed them with his blessing. Father Anchieta was not only a friend and protector of animals. He also used the wonderful power that God had given him over them to keep them from doing any damage; and more than once the inhabitants of the countries in which he was preaching the Gospel had recourse to him in these circumstances. At the first signal he made the animals obey him, but took care to employ no other means than kindness. Thus one day, when he was living in the district of the Holy Spirit, he made a monkey obey him in a wonderful manner. This monkey had for a long time devastated a neighbouring plantation of sugar-canes. In vain was the animal watched and snares laid; it escaped the most careful watchfulness. Constantly, even in the daytime, it did some fresh harm, and the keeper only arrived in time to receive a superfine grimace. Weary of the struggle, the planter had recourse to St. Anchieta. The Saint went to the plantation, and the monkey came up at once, as if on the look-out for him; but, instead of rushing through the sugar-canes, as he generally did, he came humbly to the father, who thus gently remonstrated with him: " What you do is not good, because it is thieving, and no one is permitted to thieve. I forbid you, moreover, in future to touch this plantation. When you wish for something to eat, come back if you like, but be careful to wait until you are given something." The monkey went away quietly, to the astonishment of those present. He came back afterwards to the plantation, but did no damage. He only gained by the new procedure, for he soon became a favourite with the planter, who never allowed him to want anything.

St. Josse, whose cultus was formerly so great in France, and even in Germany, renounced the rule over a great part of Brittany to adopt a religious life. He is Patron of Ponthieu. While working one day in the field he came across a hare, which not only did not escape from him, but allowed tself to be quietly caught. And when his companion wanted to kill it, he said, " Brother, if it has done no harm—nay, rather, has trusted itself to us—why should we injure it?" And so he gave it its freedom, and let it go. Shortly afterwards, while flying from huntsmen who were pursuing it, it ran straight to the man of God, and he quickly hid it in the sleeve of his coat until the huntsmen had gone away, and then let it go. Consequently, the blessed Saint is usually represented with a hare in his sleeve. Sometimes a little bird slipped in through the window, and readily flew to his hand and nestled in it.

Of St. Anthony, the Hermit, and his hog, Mrs. Jameson says that the idea prevailed that he had taken the unclean animals specially under his protection, and that for this cause is he represented with the hog in Catholic art.

Poetical justice is done to animals by various Catholic writers. Of the exquisite verses of Mrs. Katharine Tynan Hinkson concerning St. Francis and his brothers and sisters among dumb creatures (*Ballads and Lyrics*, Bullen), one specimen appears at the beginning of this book; and in Canada the same note has been sounded by Father John Bannister Tabb, a note at once fanciful and profound. (Poems: By John Bannister Tabb. Selected by Mrs. Meynell. Burns and Oates). These are two of his poems:

HOLY GROUND.

Pause where apart the fallen sparrow lies,
   And lightly tread;
For there the pity of a Father's eyes
   Enshrines the dead.

THE LAMB-CHILD.

When Christ the Babe was born,
   Full many a little lamb
Upon the wintry hills forlorn
   Was nestled near its dam;

And, waking or asleep,
   Upon His Mother's breast,
For love of her, each mother sheep
   And baby-lamb He blessed.

ACKNOWLEDGMENTS.

The gratitude of the PUBLISHERS of this book is due to the authors of *L'Eglise et la Pitié envers les Animaux*—an anonymous English gentleman and the MARQUISE DE RAMBURES; for of that book the present work offers, if not an exact translation, at least an adaptation. The unselfish labour of the adapter requires also a word of warm thanks.

During the passage of the book through the Press, the Publishers have been greatly encouraged by an incident, which is thus recorded in the *Athenæum:*—

"POPE PIUS X., who is lending a favourable countenance to movements in Italy for the Prevention of Cruelty to Animals, mostly of English initiation, has just accepted, with high approval, *L'Eglise et la Pitié envers les Animaux*. A translation of this work, which illustrates the amiable relations between animals and certain Saints and Doctors of the Church, is about to be published by Messrs. BURNS & OATES.

Thanks are also due to the Authors, Publishers, and Editors, who have graciously permitted the use of extracts from their works: His Eminence CARDINAL CAPECELATRO; ARCHBISHOP BAGSHAWE (formerly Bishop of Nottingham); ABBOT OF MONTE-CASSINO; MONSIGNORS LANDSTEINER and MOYES; FATHERS LESCHER and NEVILLE; Mesdames OZANAM, LAPORTE, and ABEL RAM; the HON. STEPHEN COLERIDGE; the VISCOUNT DE MEAUX; ARCHBISHOP RYAN; The PRIOR OF THE GRANDE CHARTREUSE; DOM HUNTER BLAIR, Bart., O.S.B.; The CURÉ OF SAINT SULPICE; Mrs. HINKSON and the Rev. DR. HENRY.

www.ingramcontent.com/pod-product-compliance
Lightning Source LLC
Chambersburg PA
CBHW022101160426
43198CB00008B/312